New Ways to
Reach the Kids
You Care About
in These
Uncertain Times

Saving the
Millennial
Generation

Dawson McAllister
with Pat Springle

THOMAS NELSON PUBLISHERS
Nashville

Published in Nashville, Tennessee, by Thomas Nelson, Inc.

The Bible version used in this publication is THE NEW KING JAMES VER-SION. Copyright © 1979, 1980, 1982, Thomas Nelson, Inc., Publishers.

Library of Congress Cataloging-in-Publication Data

McAllister, Dawson.

Saving the millennial generation : new ways to reach the kids you care about in these uncertain times / Dawson McAllister with Pat Springle.

p.   cm.

Includes bibliographical references.

ISBN 0-7852-8296-3 (pbk.)

1. Church work with youth—United States.   I. Springle, Pat, 1950–
II. Title

BV4447.M353   1999

259'.2—dc21

98-51359
CIP

Printed in the United States of America.

3 4 5 6   04 03 02 01 00

Contents

Acknowledgments v

1. After the Xers 1
2. Continental Shifts 15
3. Windows 31
4. Eroded Trust 52
5. Information Without Wisdom 62
6. Truth? Who Cares? 70
7. Isolation, Fragmentation, and Drift 80
8. 4-N Language 89
9. Real Spirituality 100
10. Hold Fast to the Truth 111
11. The Challenges of Discipling the Millennial
     Generation 123
12. Making the Church Work for Millennials 137
13. 4-N Missions 148
14. The Challenge of Parenting the Millennial Generation 155
15. And Tomorrow 164
    Appendix: Sunday School Class or
       Group Leader's Guide 172
    Notes 183
    About the Author 186

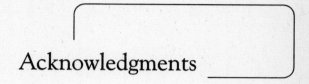

Acknowledgments

Thanks to . . .

Dr. Rich Tompkins of the Medical Institute for Sexual Health in Austin, Texas, for providing his organization's research about the sexual habits of Millennials.

Craig Davis and John Haddad for giving input from their ministries to Millennials.

Kristi LaMell, assistant high school principal, for sharing her observations about the changes in secondary education in the past twenty years.

Don Sapaugh for believing in this book and helping to get it off the ground.

1

After the Xers . . .

Several years ago, I scheduled a speaking engagement in Canada. It was my first time in that country, and I was shocked at how different the culture was from American culture. I had trouble getting through Customs because the Canadian officer saw my Bible and wondered if I was from some cult. I was shocked that the officer raised such a stink simply because I had a Bible, but my bigger shock occurred during the first talk that week. No matter what funny stories I told, no matter how hard I worked in my talk, no matter that I tried to sit with the kids in the cafeteria, I went through an ordeal—because they didn't trust me. They didn't show any signs that they liked me at all. So there I was with kids who didn't like me, feeling uncomfortable and unwanted in a foreign country and culture with kids who weren't getting it.

On the fourth day, everything changed. They warmed up— and when they warmed up, they *really* warmed up. They finally realized that I cared, that I was going to be there, and that I wasn't backing off.

Years later I had the opportunity to go to Canada a second time, and I told myself there is a four-day rule: expect nothing the first four days because they are studying you to decide whether or not they trust you. Little did I know that in just a matter of a few years, American teenagers would respond the same way. Today, everywhere I go, teenagers have the attitude: "I don't trust you, but I want to trust you, so please don't let me down. I'm going to test you and wait and see if you really mean what you say."

Others have noticed this phenomenon in their ministries. Not long ago, several of us had lunch together to talk about youth ministry. A youth pastor shook his head as he told me how his ministry had changed: "A few years ago, it took about six weeks for junior high students to trust me. The seventh graders came up in early September, and by mid-October, they felt relaxed. They listened to what I had to say. It's different now. In the past couple of years, it has taken about six *months* for them to trust me."

He leaned back in his chair, mulling over the implications of the change, then he continued, "It's the same thing at camps. We used to tell counselors to expect the high school students to take about twenty-four hours to warm up to them. But now that doesn't happen during the entire camp. And if you don't connect with these kids . . ." His voice trailed off. It was obvious what he left unsaid.

Several of us continued to talk about how youth ministry had changed over the past few years. We came to a consensus: students today are slower to trust than ever in our memories. To put it another way, these students are more analytical and skeptical of conventional "truth"—and the people who try to communicate that truth—than any students we've ever seen.

The inability or unwillingness to trust is just one characteristic of the new generation of young people, but it is perhaps the most significant, especially in terms of how they evaluate truth shared by others and how they assimilate values into their lives.

For years, sociologists—and marketing experts—have focused on the Baby Boomers and Generation Xers. The new generation after the Xers, called the Millennial Generation because of its proximity to the turn of the thousand-year mark, is in some ways a continuation of a trend. But in other ways, Millennials are a breed apart, and we who care about them need to be aware of these differences if we hope to shape their futures or even relate to them at all. Perhaps the most often-quoted recent book dealing with generations is *The Fourth Turning* by William Strauss and Neil Howe. Their analysis of the Boomers and Xers is particularly helpful. My observations, however, differ somewhat from their views of the Millennials. For the sake of context, let's take a brief look at the history and characteristics of Boomers, Xers, and Millennials.

BOOMERS

Most sociologists identify Boomers as people born between the end of World War II (1945) and 1964. (Strauss and Howe give 1943–60 as the dates for Boomer births, probably because these dates fit with their larger picture of cyclical history.) Children during this period of our history lived through the early years of the cold war when the threat of Soviet nuclear missiles was very real. The kids were the first generation to have their own identity as teenagers. In all the centuries previous to the Boomers, individuals passed from childhood to adulthood as soon as possible. Farm and industrial labor needed to be done. There simply wasn't the luxury of letting capable, available kids spend their time growing through puberty. The Jewish rite of bar mitzvah ushers male children into the responsibilities of full adulthood at age thirteen. Many other cultures had (or have) similar rituals. The concept of leisured youth took hold after World War II, and the term *teenagers* became part of the popular vocabulary around the same time. Teenagers became an identifiable group of people, and they basked in the newfound wealth and attention of postwar America. The prosperity of the '50s coincided with strong families, community friendliness, and rapid suburban growth. Television shows that represent this generation of families include *Leave It to Beaver* and *Father Knows Best.*

The most significant historical moment of this generation

was the assassination of President Kennedy. Almost every Boomer can tell you when and how he heard the news that November day in 1963. In fact, some people say that event marked the end of American naïveté and the advent of new, powerful, disruptive forces in our country. The years just after Kennedy's death saw civic upheaval in the civil rights movement and the protests against the Vietnam War. Cities all across the nation were burned in urban violence. The extremes of the movements included the Black Panthers, Weathermen, and Kent State riots. Family values got turned upside down with the hippie movement's embrace of free sex and hard drugs, but on its coattails came one of the greatest awakenings in church history: the Jesus movement.

As the Boomers matured and entered the workforce, a startling transformation took place. The flower child hippies became consumer-oriented, ladder-climbing young adults. They were called yuppies: young urban professionals. In U.S. business and politics, the leaders from the GI and the Silent Generations were only recently shouldered from power. George Bush, a fighter pilot in the Pacific theater of World War II, was the last of his era to hold the White House. After him came a pair of Boomers as president and vice president: Clinton and Gore.

Boomers are get-it-done people who believe they can control the world. They are characterized by terms such as "idealistic, manipulative, flashy and headstrong."[1]

XERS

Generation X children were born between 1965 and 1981 (Strauss and Howe cite 1961–81). During the first years of this generation's childhood and early adolescence, the Vietnam War ground to a close, civil rights legislation was enacted, and blacks made great strides toward normalizing Dr. King's dream (though it is still not fully realized). Man first set foot on the moon in 1969.

For many, the most significant events of these years were Watergate and President Nixon's resignation in disgrace.

Divorce rates soared during these years, and as always, children suffered. Coupled with divorce, the Boomers' preoccupation with themselves, first through drugs and sex and later through corporate ladder-climbing and consumption, made child raising less than a priority to them. Millions of children came home from school to empty homes because their mothers held jobs to pay the bills. These children were called latchkey kids, a reference to the unwanted and unsupervised offspring in a Dickens novel. Estimates are that 25 percent of children ages six to twelve in the United States in 1982 were latchkey kids, seven million children.[2] Movies became more violent and overtly sexual. The most common rating for movies moved from G or PG to R.

Technology exploded during these years. The space program fueled some of this growth, but the private sector quickly learned to use, and then to advance, this knowledge. Only a decade after the first moon landing in 1969, the average car had more computer memory than that landing craft.

Free sex was popularized during the '60s, but sex was never more popular than in the proliferation of sexual experiences during the '70s and '80s. Banner headlines blared "Children Having Children" and reported a million teen pregnancies each year. STDs (sexually transmitted diseases) spread like wildfire, and so did the greatest medical scourge to come from these years: AIDS.

Xers were widely characterized as slackers by the Boomers (who obviously had forgotten their love for Woodstock, Haight-Ashbury, free love, and pot), but Xers are proving to be very capable employees as they enter the business world. The tradition of corporate loyalty gradually has given way, however, to a free agency approach in which Xers market their skills to the highest bidder.

Xers are not idealists like their predecessors. They are suspicious and pragmatic.

MILLENNIALS

Many sociologists identify the first of this new generation, the Millennials, as the high school class of 2000, or children born in and after 1982. The "Reagan revolution" has brought unprecedented prosperity (at least until this writing) to our country. The cold war ended with the demolition of the Berlin Wall and the breakup of the old Soviet Union into separate states. The United States now reigns as the only superpower, though that power seems to be less than effective in curtailing some regional bullies such as Saddam Hussein of Iraq.

As a reaction to the Silent Generation's self-possessed parenting of Boomer kids and the detached parenting of Xers, parents of Millennials appear to be much more attentive. Government policies and initiatives have focused on the needs of children in recent years, including a rating system for television programs and a proposal for V-chips to install in televisions so that parents can eliminate unwanted shows. Strauss and Howe note that movies depicting children have swung from the extreme of the devil child (*The Exorcist*) in the last generation to children as angels or being led by angels today (*Angels in the Outfield*). As we will see in subsequent chapters of this book, these efforts may not be as effective as parents and lawmakers hope. Other, powerful forces undermine these attempts to protect Millennial children.

Culturally, the lack of a national cause has allowed our society to fragment into interest groups based on race, ethnicity, economic status, and virtually any other identifiable feature. This fragmentation leaves us with less of a sense of national identity, with no central, defining cause to rally around.

If we thought technology advanced during the last generation, we will be dizzy at the pace of technology development today! Every computer seems as fast as lightning one day, but is quickly surpassed by newer, much faster machines. The old "slow" computers are then discarded by impatient users. The life of new computer software is often measured in months, not years.

The pace of technological development is matched by the incredible rapidity of images on television, movies, and any visual media. To see the difference, watch a program from the '70s and notice how the characters and the plot seem to be mired in molasses. MTV, commercials, and any media for young people must contain a succession of rapid-fire images, or it is considered old and out of date. For Boomers, change was a mandate. They were out to change the world. Change was threatening to Xers who felt unsafe and unstable in the world the Boomers created for them. Millennials, however, thrive on change. It is the air they breathe, and the more of it, the better. All of us are breathing this air, but the Millennials enjoy it. Many of the rest of us gasp.

This quick pace of life today, however, doesn't make us happier. We have many more options to spend our money, we move more quickly from one place to another, but civility and relationships suffer. One snapshot of our culture is the widespread road rage on our streets. People are angry, and the cultural boundaries on expressing that anger are coming down—to our shame and at our risk.

The great social causes of the '60s and early '70s atrophied during the Me Generation '80s. Today, few, if any, national causes grip the souls and stir the emotional fires of our young people.

Here is a quick description of Millennials:

- They are plugged in. Students use computers as a way of life. That's where they do their homework, research term papers, contact their friends, and play games. In addition, Millennials use other electronics such as televisions and CD players far more than any generation ever. This absorption into the technological world comes at a price. Millennials have poor verbal skills because they don't talk to people as much as previous generations did.

- They are passionately tolerant. I met with a group of students recently and asked them if their school promotes tolerance. They gave me an earful! They said they are ridiculed for saying Christ—or anything else—is truth "because you can't know, and even if you did, you shouldn't hurt anybody's feelings." "In fact," one of the students told me, "people are tolerant of everything . . . except absolutes." Millennials are so focused on not condemning any concept that they have lost any sense of purpose for their generation. Their only cause is not making waves.

- They are spiritual, but without focus. The good news is that today's students are very god-conscious. The bad news is, they don't know which god to pursue. This phenomenon ties in with the lack of absolutes. If they have no objective way of determining truth, then one spiritual concept is as good as any other. Their hunger for God is satisfied if they get into relationships that model the love and truth of Christ, but there are many counterfeits.

- They are not quick to trust adults. They live in the most affluent society of all time, but Millennials don't trust the ones who provide for them, teach them, protect them, and minister to them. Some complain that their Boomer parents give them too much without understanding their hopes and fears. Others complain that their teachers, parents, and other adults are too preoccupied with themselves, and still others point to the sins of their fathers and condemn them for being poor role models.

The lack of trust is the salient issue of this generation. It shapes how they relate to authority, how they perceive truth, and what direction they have—or don't have—for their lives. But it also provides us with a wide door of opportunity to reach these people for whom Christ died. We have to take a good, long, hard look at ourselves as we try to minister to them, though, because, as one observer noted, "Their B.S. detectors are always on."

Maybe it's because they've seen every concei
blood, gore, crime, and violence on television or
but students today aren't shocked by many things at all. Rape?
Yeah, it happens. Oral sex in the school parking lot at lunch?
Sure. Happens every day. Cheating? You gotta be kidding. All day
every day.

In their book about reaching Generation X for Christ, *Inside
the Soul of a New Generation,* Tim Celek and Dieter Zander outline
the differences between Boomers and Xers.[3] I add Millennials to
their chart:

BOOMERS	XERS	MILLENNIALS
Conquer	Connect	Fragmented
Get ahead	Get along	Get away
Product	Process	Information
Live to work	Work to live	Live to know
Innovative	Adaptive	Analytical
Job first	Family & friends first	Niche group first
Trust demanded	Trust earned	Trust eroded

The chart depicts the monumental changes that have
occurred in American society in the past forty to fifty years. In the
scope of history, this time frame is very short, but those of us who
live during a span like this may not even notice changes until we
step back and reflect. Boomers are idealistic and have the bravado
to conquer space, technology, politics, and virtually any other
challenge. Xers are not so idealistic, but they value relationships.
For Millennials, relationships have fragmented into competing
niche groups. This trend is reflected in the Boomers' goal of getting ahead, the Xers' goal of getting along, and the Millennials' goal
of getting away. Boomers value the product, the end goal, the bottom line. Xers, on the other hand, are more absorbed in the
process of getting there. Millennials are enamored with all the
sources of information comprising that process. The generations

re becoming more narrow in focus. That funnel shows up in work styles: Boomers live to work, Xers work to live, and Millennials live to know.

As the leading edge of the technology revolution, Boomers have been tremendously innovative in experimenting with and charting new courses. Xers have become the custodians of those innovations as they have learned to adapt the changes to new applications. Millennials, so far at least, seem to be highly analytical about the uses of technology. Time will tell if they use their knowledge to find bold, new paths or if they are content to find applications for existing technology. Boomers have been focused on being upwardly mobile; their yuppie mentality has been to climb the corporate ladder at all costs. Xers have reacted to the destructive nature of the Boomers' preoccupation with work, and they typically value relationships more than jobs. Again, we don't yet know how Millennials will respond, but already we see two trends: they are intensely loyal to their own niche group, and they are committed to working so that they can have the material things they want. Perhaps we are seeing Millennials blend the values of their parents and grandparents in this regard.

One of the most striking changes in the generations is their willingness to trust. The supreme confidence of Boomers has made them demand the trust of others. Xers are not so confident. Their growing skepticism has caused them to realize that trust must be earned. The erosion of confidence hits a new low among the current generation of young people. It appears that for an alarming number of them at least, trust has eroded almost to the point of hopelessness. Recent surveys report that young people today are the first generation in this century without the belief that their lives will be better than their parents'. This statistic is only the tip of the iceberg. The erosion of trust has filtered into virtually every relationship and every environment: home, school, media, friendships, and church.

You may be reading these characteristics of the Millennial

Generation—the lack of trust, passionate tolerance, unfocused spirituality, and pervasive use of technology—and you may be thinking, *That's not my child (or my youth group or my class)!* The description of the Millennials is not of a particular person or a few people. It is an analysis of the youth culture as a whole. There are, of course, many exceptions, just as there were plenty of people in the '70s who didn't engage in free love or use LSD. We are looking at the pattern of this generation. We are examining the trends, and they are alarming!

Not long ago, *Group,* a magazine about youth ministry, asked several prominent Americans to comment on how the youth culture had changed in the past twenty years (roughly a generation). Here are their observations:

George Gallup (co-chairman of the Gallup Organization)

The past 20 years have brought more of humanity's blessings and burdens into the minds and onto the shoulders of teenagers. An explosion of communications technology left few of the world's secrets untold, and, as usual, young people learned faster than their elders.

A few television networks have given way to hundreds of channels that soon may number thousands. Almost any kind of information can be received at almost any time, and anywhere. Through satellite communications, today's teen may know more about events in Bosnia than in Boston. Millions of young people soar through cyberspace to exchange experiences on personal computers, and pace cars on the information superhighway are driven by teenagers. As a result, there are few local fads in the teenage global village.

It is no doubt impossible to judge the total impact of the communications revolution on teenagers. What is certain, however, is that it has brought them more fully into the global society and given them a larger share of the perils and pleasures of their time.

Wayne Rice (co-founder of Youth Specialties)

Today's kids don't have the support systems that were in place 20 years ago. The loss of the two-parent nuclear family and the extended family as a given of childhood has had an enormous impact on the well-being and healthy development of kids. They are more alone, more dependent upon each other, and have a more difficult time making decisions and answering questions of identity and purpose. That's one reason why the best youth ministry today is very relational, very family-oriented.

Martin Marty (author, speaker, professor of modern Christianity at the University of Chicago, senior editor for *The Christian Century* magazine)

The biggest impact is the flow and flood of impulses from all directions—peers, school, TV, and advertising. These have always been there, but the difference between 20 years ago and now is that there are fewer filters, fewer fortifications. There's less intactness to the family, to the clubs, to the after-school activities in high school, to the church youth group, to the neighborhood—to all of these elements that used to make it possible for parents to help screen the worst from the adolescent. There are fewer instruments that would help [young people] interpret what's coming their way.

Neil Howe (co-author of *The Fourth Turning*)

I would say probably the biggest shift [in the last two decades] would be worries about upward economic mobility. In [the '70s], young people's expectations were still unbelievably optimistic about the future. Now, everybody talks about money—even in junior high school.

Households under age 30 have lost about 15 percent in household income to inflation in the last 20 years. There has been an enormous divergence in the economic fortunes of older and younger Americans. The last several years have been very difficult for graduating seniors. A lot of people realized they'd played everything by the rules—they went to college, they got the degrees, they worked hard. But there was just nothing out there for them. They ended up driving a UPS truck. That's sobering, and I think that reality has filtered down to high school.

George Barna (founder and president of the Barna Research Group and author of several books, including *Frog in the Kettle*)
    Among the most critical changes [in the last 20 years] have been:

1. The dramatic increase in the number of lifestyle choices available to kids.

2. The reduction in the number and understanding of moral and ethical absolutes and limitations.

3. The quickening of response time in decision-making, resulting in spontaneous decisions based on minimal reflection.

4. The substantial surge in the volume of information available—quite conveniently and inexpensively—on a vast array of topics.

5. The lowered personal standards concurrent to the heightened level of expectations we have of other people and institutions.

6. The increase in stress and anxiety, along with the decrease in hope and joy.

7. The deterioration of the family as a stable base of support.

8. The demise of other social institutions focused upon providing support for young people.

9. And an exceedingly intrusive and opinionated media which passes along its own biases as objective reporting.

(Reprinted by permission from GROUP Magazine, copyright 1994, Group Publishing, Box 481, Loveland, CO 80539.)[4]

In these pages, we will take a closer look at how the culture has changed over the past few generations (and we might have a couple of laughs in the process). We'll focus on the main characteristics of the Millennials to understand them well, and then we'll focus on ways to communicate the love and life-changing power of God to these dear young people. No generation is comfortable with those who follow it. For reasons we'll examine in later chapters, that statement may be more true today than ever before, but we need to face our fears and put aside our "right to be right." Relating to Millennials requires insight, patience, and a big dose of love. Some of us (okay, most of us!) will have to change so that we can relate to them. No, I don't mean we have to change what we believe. If anything, we need to be clearer and stronger about what we believe! But we need to change how we relate, how we communicate our values and truth, so these young people will listen. You and I have a tremendous challenge if we want God to use us to minister and parent today's students. We'd better pay attention to what's going on, or we may lose them. That's too high a price to pay for feeling that our way is right!

2

Continental Shifts

Geologists tell us that millions of years ago, all the continents were one land mass called Pangaea. Over the eons, Africa drifted south, North and South America drifted west, and Australia moved inexorably to the southeast. The continental plates, they tell us, continue to move a few inches each year. Although this process seems slow to us, it is responsible for the identifiable shape of the continents and oceans on earth today. And the collisions of these plates are the causes of towering mountain ranges such as the Himalayas, earthquakes in the Pacific rim, and volcanoes around the globe. Now I realize that some of us may believe in a recent creation, and this talk of continental shifts sounds like Darwinian baloney! But some of us also believe in God's creation of the earth millions—or even billions—of years ago.

In case you didn't know it, this book is not Geology 101, but the theory of continental drifting is a good illustration of what has happened to our culture. We can look at our society today and wonder, "What happened? How did we get here? Not long ago, families watched *Leave It to Beaver* together. Now the kids watch things I don't even want to know about!" Let's examine the seemingly slow, but genuinely cataclysmic forces that shape our culture today.

POSTMODERN/POST-CHRISTIAN

Among sociologists like Strauss and Howe, and Christian commentators who are writing about Generation X, it is almost gospel to depict postmodernism as the overarching wave of modern history. In many ways, I think these authorities are correct. Postmodern culture is a major shift in Western culture, the type of change that happens only every several hundred years or so. Postmodernism follows the dominant cultural wave of the last three and a half centuries: the Enlightenment. Some commentators identify the last three cultural movements in Western culture as the Protestant Reformation (1500 to 1700), the Enlightenment (1600 to 1960), and postmodernism (1960 to ?). We should note that modernism is the period of Western history from the mid-fifteenth century to the modern era. During the Renaissance, the ruling and educated classes gained the increasing perception that they could, by reason and self-will, alter the course of their lives and their civilizations. This perception found its high-water mark in the Enlightenment, when it was believed that man's reason and ingenuity could solve virtually every problem.

The Protestant Reformation focused on the dignity of the individual, salvation by faith, and the authority of Scripture. It began in Germany with Martin Luther, then swept northern Europe and America with the commitment to the powerful combination of freedom and faith. The truth of the Scriptures provided the anchor of absolutes for decision making, political reforms, and lifestyle. Anselm's statement, "I believe in order that I may understand," is the philosophy of that age.

The Enlightenment overlapped the Reformation period, and it has lasted up to the modern period. Early Enlightenment philosophers were not attempting to undermine faith in God. Philosopher René Descartes was a Christian who wanted to use human reason to strengthen his faith in Christ. In his book *Generating Hope,* Jimmy Long observes,

To accomplish this task, Descartes developed the principle of doubt through the use of human reason. From this beginning he coined the phrase, "I think, therefore I am." He believed self-knowledge was the foundation on which all knowledge could be built. As a result, human reason usurped God as the basis for all knowledge. What I think, not what God reveals, becomes the measure of truth.[1]

Descartes's good intentions ultimately led to the anchor of truth being yanked from the solid sea floor and tossed away. Truth became relative. Reason prevailed, but that reason was too often flawed to be a foundation for values and relationships, and it certainly did not point people to God.

In recent years, reason itself has come under attack. All the carefully crafted philosophies of the Enlightenment have disintegrated into what Long calls "the shifting sandcastle of Postmodernism." The industrial revolution of the Enlightenment period opened new opportunities for wealth and life, but the technology revolution of the past few decades has gone much farther. It has brought far more opportunities, but it has contributed to the undermining of values and relationships. Vaclav Havel, president of the Czech Republic, stated, "We live in the Postmodern world where everything is possible and almost nothing is certain. The abyss between the rational and the spiritual, the external and the internal, the objective and the subjective, the technical and the moral, the universal and the unique, constantly grows deeper."[2]

This chart describes the contrasts between the Enlightenment era and our postmodern period:[3]

ENLIGHTENMENT	POSTMODERNISM
Truth	Preference
Reason	Experience
Autonomous self	Community
Scientific discovery	Virtual reality

| Human progress | Human misery |
| Optimism | Pessimism |

Today, students not only are unaware of truth; many of them simply don't see any relevance of propositional truth. They value tolerance and regard absolutes as backward, narrow, and uncaring. Reason and careful reflection don't determine a person's course of action. Instead, feelings and experience shape the course of young lives. The freedom of the individual that was the cornerstone of democratic political movements throughout the world, such as the American Revolution, has shifted. Now freedoms are taken for granted, and people sense a need for community as the world fragments around them. Recent centuries have witnessed unprecedented scientific discoveries in every field, and those discoveries continue today. Yet our fascination has shifted to experiences that are not quite real; they are created on computers: virtual reality. The past two or three hundred years have seen incredible changes in humanitarian outreach. Slaves were freed, missionary movements swept the globe, and in relatively recent years, the Marshall Plan saved war-ravaged Europe from catastrophic starvation. But where are the great movements today to relieve the suffering of people in our country and throughout the world?

By and large, we are too preoccupied with our own comfort to care. In years past, people had almost limitless enthusiasm and optimism for making life better. In one of the most staggering statistics of the depression era, a majority of people suffering devastating conditions still felt that life would be better soon. In contrast, although today we have the most affluent culture ever known, young people have a strange, pervasive sense of foreboding about their lives and the future.

Commentators seem to look back on the Enlightenment as the good old days when truth was upheld and values were honored. Christians look at the effects of the postmodern culture and rightly decry the moral and ethical slide. But something doesn't ring true to me about looking back at the Enlightenment and wishing for its return. Perhaps Descartes had the noblest intentions when he embarked on his path to bolster his faith through human reason, but Thomas Jefferson was also a child of the Enlightenment. A brilliant man and one of the founders of our democratic republic, he didn't advance the cause of Christ. A friend of mine told me that his great-aunt died a few years ago and left him a Jefferson Bible. My friend was excited to get it, but as he read familiar accounts in the Gospels, he noticed something was missing. Actually a lot of things were missing! Jefferson had excised every mention of a miracle and every statement about the deity of Christ. He thought the moral teachings of Jesus were worthy of study and reflection, but the authority of Scripture about the central issue of Christ's being the Messiah to pay for sins was too much for his "enlightened" mind. He just cut out "offending" passages.

Recently I pulled a book off my shelf I hadn't read in many years. In the mid-1980s, Francis Schaeffer wrote a prophetic book, *The Great Evangelical Disaster.* As usual, this brilliant Christian philosopher was ahead of his time. In the book, Schaeffer described the slide away from the authority of Scripture toward intellectual and moral anarchy. He warned against Christians looking too fondly back at the Enlightenment. He quoted the *Oxford Dictionary of the Christian Church* to show how the foundations of the Enlightenment and the Christian faith are polar opposites:

> The Enlightenment combines opposition to all supernatural religion and belief in the all-sufficiency of human reason with an ardent desire to promote the happiness of men in this life . . . Most of its representatives . . . rejected the Christian dogma and were hostile to Catholicism as well as Protestant orthodoxy, which they regarded as powers of spiritual darkness depriving humanity of the use of its rational faculties . . . Their fundamental belief in the goodness of human nature, which blinded

them to the fact of sin, produced an easy optimism and absolute faith of human society once the principle of enlightened reason has been recognized. The spirit of the Enlightenment penetrated deeply into German Protestantism [in the nineteenth century], where it disintegrated faith in the authority of the Bible and encouraged Biblical criticism on the one hand and an emotional "Pietism" on the other.[4]

The Enlightenment doesn't comprise the good old days for Christians. During these centuries of emphasis on self and reason, biblical truth was slowly, steadily undermined. Many Christian scholars believe the real turning point occurred in the last decades of the nineteenth century when German theologians applied their theories of "higher criticism" to Scripture. In effect, they changed the presuppositions from "the Bible is authoritative" to "miracles and the supernatural do not exist" or, at best, "we can't know what is true." Bible-believing Christians went on the defensive to protect the fundamentals of the faith. In the early decades of the twentieth century, *fundamentalist* was not a pejorative term as it is today. Then it meant someone who held fast to the authority of God's Word against the onslaught of intellectualized doubt.

Public education, championed by John Dewey, politics, media, and virtually every aspect of life were affected, and gradually Christianity retreated to pockets of the faithful instead of the faithful permeating society. Francis Schaeffer watched this slide over the course of his long life, and he was deeply grieved that "the Christian influence on the whole of culture has been lost" in Europe over many years and, in the United States, in only a short time from the 1920s to the 1960s. He wrote, "Ours is a post-Christian world in which Christianity, not only in the number of Christians but in cultural emphasis and cultural result, is no longer the consensus or ethos of our society." Schaeffer reflected on his life and lamented,

Do not take this lightly! It is a horrible thing for a man like myself to look back and see my country and my culture go down the drain in my own lifetime. It is a horrible thing that sixty years ago you could move across this country and almost everyone, even non-Christians, would have known what the gospel was. A horrible thing that fifty to sixty years ago our culture was built on the Christian consensus, and now this is no longer the case.[5]

It is sad that ours is a postmodern culture. It is tragic that it is post-Christian.

Most writers say that the Xers were the first truly postmodern generation. The perspectives of postmodernism are more established and normalized for the Millennials, but some still refuse to believe it is real. Josh McDowell's best-selling book, *Right from Wrong,* addressed today's slide from absolutes into the swamp of relativism. Thousands of churches benefited from his book, workbooks, and videos for teenagers and their parents, yet Josh received criticism from some sources for being too global and too alarmist. Did Josh ever exaggerate to make a point? No, I believe his analysis of the culture was based on painstaking research. Did he generalize his findings? Of course. That's what a social commentator does. Is he an alarmist? Yes, because the present situation calls for a loud, clear alarm!

PARENTS

The good news is that parents today are more attentive and concerned about their children than they have been in many years. The bad news is that their efforts are often overshadowed by forces beyond their control. Today's teenagers are the children of late Boomer and early Xer parents. Early Boomer permissiveness with Xer children has changed dramatically. Today's parents have reacted against the inattention given to Xers. "Family values" is the number one issue in many political campaigns. William Bennett's *Book of Virtues* became one of the top sellers as some in our society have turned their attention back to core values.

In the workplace, a revolution has taken place. The Boomer mentality of putting the job first has given way to telecommuting and job sharing so that parents can spend more time with their children. Parents are making sure someone is there when the children get home from school. Two-thirds of working parents said they would accept lower pay for more time with their families.

The divorce rate, which skyrocketed in the previous decades, has now stabilized. The abortion rate has followed suit. Both statistics reflect a moderating of the forces that destabilized the family over the last generation. The commitment to family and God is reflected also in the popularity of the Million Man March in Washington, D.C., and the many Promise Keepers conferences and rallies across the country. In both, men are asked to pledge themselves to right living, faith in God, and the honor of their commitment to their families, no matter what the cost. National news programs showed men making these public professions, often with tears of sincerity and often with their children by their sides or on their shoulders. The sheer size of these events is the measure of how deeply they have struck a chord in men's lives.

Still, even in light of the monumental change of direction in parents' attention toward children, many Millennials feel isolated. They are independent, trusting only in themselves for direction and motivation, and they resent any connection with the slacker image of the Xers. One teenager summed up the perspective of many of his peers: "I know that the only person that is going to accomplish my dreams is me. If we don't seem to have any motivation, it's because our parents have been so lenient in saying, 'Do your own thing.' But we know we have to do things for ourselves."[6]

Parents can do a lot to nurture their children. The family has been, is, and will remain the strongest influence on the lives of young people. But conservative, Christian parents today have to realize they are battling uphill against the onslaught of the insidious, pervasive, postmodern, post-Christian culture that steeps kids in relativism and undermines truth as the foundation for their lives.

EDUCATION

Our schools' approach to the Millennials contains both form and substance. As parents and government become more conservative and child-conscious, many schools now require kids to wear uniforms. Ostensibly uniforms take the place of gang-related clothing or high-cost, trendy outfits, but studies also show that uniforms increase student productivity and consequently grades rise. (Most teenagers, however, dispute these findings!)

Many school systems are in a "back to basics" mode. Experimentation with curriculum is out; the three Rs are in—with the addition of emphases on sciences and computers. As a result, SAT scores have risen for the first time in almost two decades. Strauss and Howe report,

> Nearly all school systems are trying to heed Rudolph Giuliani's demand that schools "once again train citizens." The new 1990s educational buzz-words call for *collaborative* (rather than independent) learning for *regular* (rather than ability-grouped) kids who must be taught *core values,* do *good works,* and meet standards, with *zero tolerance* for misbehavior. The new three R's are rules, respect, and responsibility.[7]

Surveys report that teachers feel a new sense of pride in their profession. Many are staying in their jobs longer, and the number of students entering the field of education has increased dramatically since the middle of the '80s.

Schools, however, are chief proponents and disseminators of postmodern philosophies. *Tolerance* is the watchword in classes and in the halls. Any belief is accepted—as long as it is not demanded of anyone else. This is seen most frequently in references to teen sex, abortions, and homosexuality, which are said to be accepted norms of society, and people who dispute that claim are castigated as narrow, old-fashioned and, worst of all, intolerant.

GOVERNMENT PROGRAMS

Parents' interest in the welfare of their children has not been lost on politicians (who need these parents' votes). The last decade has seen a proliferation of local, state, and national programs for the welfare of children. Many new laws have been enacted to protect children from child abuse. Legislatures across the country have rigorously pursued "deadbeat dads" to get them to pay child support. The focus on the welfare of children grew to such prominence that New York Governor Mario Cuomo dubbed the '90s the Decade of the Child. On the national agenda, presidential campaigns often focused on children by addressing schools, welfare, abuse, and violence in the media.

One of the hottest topics in the past few years has been the debate about, and then the assimilation of, the ratings system for television shows. This system was designed to inform parents so they can screen shows that might not be suitable for their children, but most families disregard the information. (And I suspect that children look at the ratings to see which shows might stimulate them the most!) The debate over the V-chip has cooled a bit, but it may surface again as the next presidential election looms. The chip will enable parents to eliminate entire categories of programming (based on the ratings) from their children's television menu rather than only advising them (based on the current ratings system).

Government-backed drug prevention programs are very popular in schools, and many politicians are actively pursuing welfare reforms to benefit children more. However, the statistics show that the rates of poverty, drug and alcohol abuse, teen sex, teen pregnancy, and incidents of teen STDs remain alarmingly high.

INSTITUTIONAL WEAKNESS

In *The Fourth Turning,* Strauss and Howe identify the cycles of history in a repeated, predictable set of circumstances that can be traced in Western civilization from the late medieval period in the 1400s. At times, the plotting of history into cycles seems a bit contrived, but sometimes the parallels are eerie. For example, we read about widespread, concerted student protests and riots that included "boycotting classes, barricading college buildings, breaking windows, trashing the commons and chapel, setting fires around or to college buildings, beating faculty members, and whipping the president or trustees."[8] Kent State? Vietnam protests? Burning ROTC buildings throughout the country? No, the events occurred in the early nineteenth century on campuses such as the University of North Carolina, Princeton, Harvard, and Yale. Students of history can find parallels to our times in generations past.

Strauss and Howe observe four specific, identifiable, orderly periods in the cycles of history:

1. Highs—characterized by enthusiasm for a new civic order and stronger institutions.

2. Awakenings—characterized by spiritual upheaval and the establishing of new values.

3. Unravelings—characterized by a decaying civic order and a weakening of institutions.

4. Crises—characterized by secular upheaval such as economic collapse or war, when the old, crumbling civic order is replaced by a new one.

Each of these turnings lasts approximately twenty years. In our era, the "high" of optimism and prosperity occurred just after the previous crises: the Great Depression and World War II. The hippie movement, the Jesus movement, and the civil rights movement all were a part of the "awakening" in the late '60s up to about 1980. Today, we find ourselves in the third turning, the "unraveling," in which government, the church, schools, and every other major institution in our society seem more or less confused and impotent to solve the problems we face. The fourth turning, the "crisis," has yet to occur. It could be a war, an economic disaster like the Great Depression, widespread terrorism, or some other calamity. In my opinion, it is easier to look back and observe history than to look forward and predict it. For that reason, we can't anticipate the exact nature of the coming years. We can be sure that bad times will come, and we can be sure that God will still be loving and sovereign, no matter what occurs. But we can't know when or how or where the blows will fall. Our focus now is on our present culture. Strauss and Howe say we are squarely in an unraveling.

Here are some current examples of institutional weakness:

- Even with the emphasis on family-oriented legislation, the scourges of drug use, abortions, teen pregnancy, and divorce remain at or near an all-time high. The recent leveling off of these statistics is encouraging, but they have leveled off above the red line.

- Violence in our country is rampant. Every night on local news and often on national news programs, we see graphic depictions of rapes, murders, gang violence, and other crimes. "If it bleeds, it leads" is the guide.

- Free-floating anger in our land finds expression in road rage as people lay aside their inhibitions and openly vent their rage for being temporarily inconvenienced. Where is patience? Where is common civility?

- George Bush brilliantly drew together a coalition of nations to turn back Saddam Hussein from Kuwait, but Saddam stayed in power and continued to build weapons of mass destruction. Bill Clinton has vowed to stop Saddam, but so far has failed. And our allies of Bush's coalition's war effort—except Great Britain—have deserted us. Indeed, some of our most powerful and influential "allies" are actively working against our efforts.

- The church is viewed as having a shrinking role in the lives of Americans. An article in *USA Today* is titled "Few Would Turn to Clergy for Help if They Were Dying." In the article, Marilyn Elias quotes pollster George Gallup Jr.: "It's a wake-up call for American clergymen." As those polled anticipate their deaths, they see their last days as "a time of serious spiritual and emotional work," but the spiritual leaders one would expect to be trusted with these matters clearly are not.

During an unraveling, the optimism of decades of hope slowly erodes. Skepticism turns to cynicism, which evolves into genuine pessimism. We aren't completely pessimistic yet. The economy is still too strong for pessimism to take root, but young people already feel the pangs of skepticism and cynicism. If the economy turns south, abject pessimism may not be far behind.

SOME CONSTANTS

Even in continental shifts, some plates stubbornly refuse to budge. They hold their place. Sometimes a neighboring plate drifts away; sometimes it crashes into the stationary one. We have looked at many sources of change in today's culture, but one thing is a constant: the nature of teenagers. They are struggling to find their identity, to find purpose and direction in life, and to be independent of their parents. That's their job description, no matter what the culture is doing around them. They want to know the answers to the questions: Who am I? Where am I going? Who cares about me? Who do I care about?

Early adolescence is characterized by very concrete thinking.

Their task is to separate facts from fantasy, and they are very black-and-white, all-or-nothing, right-or-wrong in their perceptions. In other words, they do okay with *what* questions, but they have difficulty with *why* questions because they haven't yet learned to be abstract and apply concepts to varied situations. Thirteen- to fifteen-year-olds are almost totally self-absorbed. Their bodies are changing, their hormones are raging, and they don't have a clue how to harness all the drives inside them. Their view of God is usually a grandfather type (kind, but not too bright!) or Superman (who rights every wrong and is stronger than anybody else), but they typically see spiritual motivations as simplistic: punishment if I do the wrong thing, reward if I do the right thing. They often think they can "swap marbles" with God and get Him to do what they want if they do what He wants.

Older adolescents are a different breed altogether. Girls typically enter this stage earlier than boys, but by age sixteen, both are usually at least on the threshold. At this age, their identity is much less tied to self. Their affiliation with a group determines their identity. Parents remain the single most important factor in shaping self-image and confidence, but the peer group now is much more important than in early adolescence. The thinking process becomes much more abstract and reflective. You don't have to ask *why*. They'll ask it for you! Nuances of meaning can now be discerned. (If you want to see the difference, try teaching a junior high Sunday school class sometime, then teach a high school class. You'll see!)

Spirituality is much richer and deeper in this stage of maturity. Indeed, the perceptions gained during these years often shape the person's view of God for the rest of his life. God becomes a real person who relates to the teenager like the senior member of the peer group. He is real, He is approachable, and He is God. Prayer shifts from being self- and need-focused to being much more relaxed and conversational.

Younger teenagers pick up on the mood of the culture. Their cynicism often has a hard edge to it. "That sucks" seems to be the dominant and most eloquent expression they know! They usually don't know how to process the tolerance they pick up at school and in the media because they are so black-and-white, so they become especially intolerant of anyone's lack of tolerance or they become terribly confused. If we can win their trust, however, younger teenagers are quick to absorb the wonderful (and clear) truths of God's Word.

If you don't mind wading in and having to stay wet for a while, older adolescents are a delight to talk with. You have to wade in because they will sense it if you aren't committed to relating to them in a meaningful way. And you have to stay wet for a while because you better not leave until they voice their questions and get at least an answer or two from the discussion. Their cultural cynicism, combined with adolescent insecurity and their ability to be analytical, requires that you not give them quick, simple answers. They are too sharp for that.

Underneath all the layers of cultural baggage, beneath the postmodern relativism, the governmental and parental attention that they don't necessarily buy, the skepticism and distrust, these young people desperately want to know they are loved. Those who love them have to penetrate a couple of extra layers in young people, but their hearts are just as responsive as ever to the incredible love and power of Jesus.

Sure, they can be a pain sometimes, but so were you! Don't give up on them. God hasn't. I receive thousands of calls from teenagers during each of my radio programs. (My weekly call-in radio program, *Dawson McAllister Live*, is broadcast nationwide and is one of the fastest growing Christian radio programs in the country.) Some are in big trouble with the law or with their parents. Some are just confused. And some know there is a hole in their hearts that only Jesus can fill. They all take the step of calling in because they are crying out for help.

A young man named Mario called one night and said that he was involved in a gang, and that his gang offered him love. I explained to Mario that the love of Jesus and of other believers was a different kind of love from the one his gang offered. God was working in his heart. As we talked, my words about the forgiveness of God started to break through the crust of his heart. He wanted to experience Christ, but the bonds with his gang held him back. Suddenly Mario began to cry. I told him how to pray and open his heart to Jesus, and I explained that Jesus would lead him out of the hell of his gang. He could stop having sex with his girlfriend and stop hurting people and using them. I invited him to pray along with me, and right there on national radio, Mario was born again.

Young people want to trust because God has put in each heart the desire to trust. Our whole Christian faith is based on trust. We're hard-wired to trust. If we want to communicate with them, we have to work past the pain that has caused them not to trust, and we have to speak to their deepest longings for truth, meaning, and real relationships. I am seeing more young people come to Christ today than ever before in thirty years of ministry. They want to trust, and they are taking the hand of a loving, strong, trustworthy Savior.

Millions of young people are going in the wrong direction. That wrong path is very evident for some like Mario, but many others hide their deep needs under masks of smiles and busyness. Look beneath these masks to see their longing to be loved, and love them with all your heart.

3

Windows

A friend of mine has two teenagers, one born the last year of Generation X and the other born the first year of the Millennials. As we talked about the difference in generations, we realized that it doesn't make much sense to compare two people only one year apart. The delineation of the generations is, no matter what anybody says, somewhat arbitrary. My friend said, "It's not like one grew up in one culture and the other grew up in an entirely different one." To make the changes clearer, I want to compare apples to apples, a teenager today with his counterparts at the same point in the Boomer and Xer generations. In other words, we'll examine a sixteen-year-old today with a sixteen-year-old Boomer and a sixteen-year-old Xer at the beginning of their generations. We'll look at the *real* factors that shape and reflect youth culture: music, television, movies, sex, drugs, computers, and education. If you're old enough, you might even have a few laughs in the process.

MUSIC

I asked a group of high school students, "What are your friends' favorite singers, groups, and songs today?" I stay up on the youth culture, but I'd never heard of some of the tunes they mentioned. I decided to divide the music into several categories.

Here's what they told me about drug use: "Jagged Little Pill" by Alanis Morrisette, "Fly" by Sugar Ray, "Semi-Charmed Life" (about crystal meth) by Third Eye Blind, "Budsmokers Only," by Bone Thugs-N-Harmony, and the hottest new group, Chumbawamba.

I asked them if they knew songs that promoted violence. They knew of plenty, including "Push" by Matchbox 20 (about a relationship in which the singer says, "I want to push you around"), "Bad Habit" by Offspring, "Beautiful People" and "Sweet Dreams" by Marilyn Manson, many of the rap songs, and "Pony" by Ginuwine.

And sex? That was easy: "Sex and Candy" by Marcy Playground, "Wrong Way" and "Caress Me Down" by Sublime, "Don't Fight the Feeling" by Too $hort, almost all rap songs, and "Pink" by Aerosmith.

I asked about "Pink," and one girl said, "It's about a girl who is aroused. She's getting ready to have sex. You know what I mean?"

"Yes, I think I've got it," I replied. They really got a chuckle when I told them the hottest song thirty years ago was "I Want to Hold Your Hand" by the Beatles. We've come a long way, baby!

As hard and graphic as these songs are, a softer style of music seems to be creeping into modern music: ska, which is a blend of big band and rap. According to Jill Kilcoyne of Teenage Research Unlimited, a national marketing research firm based in Northbrook, Illinois, Millennials are "distancing themselves from Xers. There's a softer edge to their music, just from where it went from rap to alternative, and now there's this little upsurge in ska music." The Mighty Mighty Bosstones wear plaid sport coats, have a guy who dances as they play, and feature a horn section, and many teenagers love them. Go figure!

If you're an Xer who was born in the mid-'60s, what popular music did you listen to? The top forty singles in your early adolescence included "You Light Up My Life" by Debby Boone, "I Just Want to Be Your Everything" by Andy Gibb, "Evergreen" by Barbra Streisand, "Dancing Queen" by Abba, "I'm Your Boogie Man" by KC and the Sunshine Band, and "Slow Dancin'" by Johnny Rivers.

The songs with sexual overtones included "Feels Like the First Time" by Foreigner, "Do You Wanna Make Love" by Peter McCann, and "Torn Between Two Lovers" by Mary MacGregor. A song about alcohol was "Margaritaville" by Jimmy Buffett.

And for the early Boomer who was born just after World War II and hit puberty around 1960, the hot songs were "Tossin' and Turnin'" by Bobby Lewis, "I Fall to Pieces" by Patsy Cline, "Michael" by the Highwaymen, "Crying" by Roy Orbison, "Runaway" by Del Shannon, "Pony Time" by Chubby Checker, "Raindrops" by Dee Clark, "Take Good Care of My Baby" by Bobby Vee, "Dedicated to the One I Love" by the Shirelles, "Where the Boys Are" by Connie Francis, "Travelin' Man" by Ricky Nelson (of *Ozzie and Harriet* fame), and "Shop Around" by the Miracles.

Perhaps the most telling statement about the music of the early '60s is that in 1961, the number 11 song for the year (which was number 1 in February of that year) was "Calcutta" by Lawrence Welk!

But a new, radical group was just getting started, singing about fun on the sand in southern California: the Beach Boys. It would be only a few more years before the Beatles, the Dave Clark Five, and Gary Puckett and the Union Gap would become popular. And during those later years, the Motown sound would bridge the racial music gap. The Four Tops, the Temptations, the Supremes, Smokey Robinson and the Miracles, Martha and the Vandellas, and Little Stevie Wonder filled jukeboxes, radios, and dance floors in white neighborhoods as well as black.

And do you remember the singer who turned the music world—and the rest of America—on its head at this time? Elvis! He came on the scene with tunes such as "Jailhouse Rock," and he gyrated his hips so much that offended television producers wouldn't show him from the waist down. His radical style also included one of the most beloved songs of that era, the romantic "Love Me Tender." Radical? In his day, sure, he was.

A few years later, in 1968, Boomer music included many new,

popular performers: "Daydream Believer" by the Monkees, "Sittin' on the Dock of the Bay" by Otis Redding, "Mrs. Robinson" (the theme from *The Graduate*) by Simon and Garfunkel, "MacArthur Park" by Richard Harris, "Hello, I Love You" by the Doors, "Hey Jude" by the Beatles, and "Those Were the Days" by Mary Hopkin.

The Graduate explored the confusion of purpose a young Boomer might experience, and its theme song, "Mrs. Robinson," evoked images of the movie's sexual encounter. But by and large, the songs of that Boomer period were still pretty tame. Haight-Ashbury, free love, drugs, and Woodstock would change all that in only a few short years.

Can you see any difference in these three snapshots of the music of these generations? What was radical years ago became incredibly lame only a few years later.

TELEVISION

I asked the teenagers what television programs their friends watch regularly. They grew up on *Power Rangers* and *Barney,* but they have graduated to more mature themes. They like many of the hip new comedies about young people in relationships. They quickly mentioned *Seinfeld, Friends,* and *The Simpsons.* They also religiously watch comedy shows such as *Saturday Night Live, Mad TV, Late Show with David Letterman, Ally McBeal,* and *Mr. Bean.*

Their taste for drama also focuses on relationships among their peers. The most common shows mentioned were *Party of Five, Seventh Heaven, Buffy the Vampire Slayer,* and *Dawson's Creek.* Casual sex is a predominant theme for these shows, both comedies and dramas. In case you aren't familiar with some of the topics the characters address, it might be instructive for you to tune in sometime. They may discuss penis sizes, intensity of orgasms, and the relative sexual performance of their friends and partners. Homosexuals are now common, not just on *Ellen,* but accepted (much more than tolerated) as members of the community. Jokes and conversations about heterosexual and homosexual experiences are the norm on prime-time television, especially in programs targeting the younger audience.

What makes these conversations so alarming to the older generations is that these conversations are so matter-of-fact—as if these are common topics of conversations in school, at the mall, or wherever teenagers meet. And they are. MTV is, of course, one of the most popular viewing preferences of this generation. The images and the songs reflect the sensuality, and often the emptiness, of this generation.

Four universities conducted a three-year survey of violence on television. The conclusion is that today's children are absorbing vast quantities of violence, which probably causes aggressive behavior. Most of the carnage in cartoons is depicted as clean and sanitized, and the good characters perpetrate 40 percent of this violence. This makes violence dangerously seductive to children. Barbara Wilson, a senior researcher and professor of communications at UC Santa Barbara, observed, "The risk here is that viewers of all ages, but especially children, are likely to emulate characters who are perceived as attractive. Younger children have difficulty distinguishing televised fantasy from reality, and are therefore at increased risk of imitating cartoon violence." About one-third of bad characters are not punished, almost three-fourths showed no remorse, and half of violent shows depicted no physical injury or pain in the victims. Negative consequences are shown in only 15 percent of the programs. The result, according to the survey, is that children are being desensitized to the damage inflicted by violence. The children whose perceptions are shaped at an early age by watching cartoons then have those notions confirmed by prime-time programming and movies that glamorize violence and show few of the genuine, devastating consequences.[1]

What did Xers watch in the middle '70s? *Charlie's Angels* and *Rockford Files* were popular, but few shows were as hot as *All in the Family* with Archie Bunker.

And the Boomers? Television was just coming into its own as the Boomers reached their teenage years. Family values were supported. Indeed, they were taken for granted. *Leave It to Beaver, Ozzie and Harriet, The Andy Griffith Show, Father Knows Best,* and of course, *I Love Lucy* were the comedy staples for most families (at least those who could afford a television). *Dragnet, Maverick, Zorro, The Untouchables,* and *Wagon Train* were popular dramas. *What's My Line* and *I've Got a Secret* were popular shows with celebrity panels. And then color television made its appearance. Suddenly the novelty of television became an obsession with American viewers. One Boomer told me, "I remember when our neighbors got a *color* television! We were amazed. They put it on their front porch so everybody in the neighborhood could come by and watch it." *The Wonderful World of Disney* made Sunday night "must see TV" for virtually every family in the nation. Disney also brought us the most popular children's show of that time: *The Mickey Mouse Club.* Today, Boomers reminisce about Annette Funicello and the sign-off: "M-I-C . . . see you real soon! K-E-Y . . . Why? Because we like you! M-O-U-S-E!"

A few years later, television had taken hold of Americans' time and attention. A list of the top shows from 1968 (when early Boomers were in their early twenties) reveals how far we'd come from those early days. The most popular comedies of 1968 included two that were considered cutting edge—*The Smothers Brothers Comedy Hour* and *Rowan and Martin's Laugh-In*—and a lot of programs that were wholesome family fun: *Green Acres, The Flying Nun, Bewitched, Gomer Pyle, USMC, My Three Sons, Hogan's Heroes, Get Smart,* and *Petticoat Junction.* Dramas of that period included: *Mission Impossible, Star Trek, It Takes a Thief, Adam 12, Wild, Wild West,* and the most beloved television program of its era, *Bonanza.*

MOVIES

In some ways, movies have changed the least over the past three generations—at least until recently. Special effects made a dramatic leap forward in the late '70s with the *Star Wars* trilogy, and since then, audiences have been titillated by increasing sophistication of techniques so that now we find ourselves "up close and personal" to lava flows, *Tyrannosaurus rex,* attacks from aliens, and explosions ad infinitum.

Millennials enjoy many of the popular movies today, such as the all-time chart topper *Titanic,* as well as *Braveheart, Men in Black, Independence Day,* and *Jurassic Park,* but they have a taste for horror, as found in *Scream* and *Scream 2.* Perhaps the most significant aspect of the Millennials' movie preferences is in their love for stupid humor. They flock to see *Dumb and Dumber, Austin Powers, Tommy Boy,* and anything by Jim Carrey (*Liar Liar, The Mask,* etc.). The law of diminishing returns continues to operate in moviegoers, and they quickly become dissatisfied unless new movies are sexier, bloodier, scarier, and "stupider," with more fantastic special effects than the last one.

Teenage Xers experienced the beginning of the craze in special effects in *Star Wars.* It is interesting to note the recent rerelease of the trilogy and see the widespread interest in the films (or videos). One striking difference in those movies and today's is that you almost never see any blood in *Star Wars,* even when Ewoks are being bashed, when Darth Vader's minions are zapped by Luke, Princess Leia, and Han Solo, or when the Empire's fighters are shooting down (or being shot by) the good guys flying for the rebels. Compare these clean, "goreless" deaths with the blood and guts of movies such as *Starship Troopers.*

But the movies of that era were not all clean and neat. Xers in their teenage years saw some of the most violent popular movies, and some of the most depressing, in cinematic history. Few audience members left the theater uplifted when they walked out of *Platoon, Apocalypse Now,* or *The Deer Hunter.* Clint Eastwood's films migrated from the high plains of the late '60s (*High Plains Drifter; The Good, the Bad, and the Ugly;* etc.) to the streets with *Dirty Harry* and a host of similar tough cop movies. The films had plenty of blood and gore for those who needed to see them. It seems that the movies of that generation were made for two distinct audiences: some for the adult Boomers who endured the violence, confusion, and protests of the Vietnam War, and some flicks for the younger Xer crowd.

Other films popular when the first Xers were in their midteens in the late '70s and early '80s included *Annie Hall, The Goodbye Girl, Heaven Can Wait, Kramer vs. Kramer, Raging Bull, The Elephant Man, Chariots of Fire, Reds,* and *Raiders of the Lost Ark.*

Younger Boomers in the early '60s saw some of the epics of film history. *Dr. Zhivago, Cleopatra,* and *Lawrence of Arabia* were long, elaborate, and immensely popular. James Dean captured the imagination of his age in *Rebel Without a Cause* and *Giant.* Marilyn Monroe made a string of films, the latter ones more forgettable as her life came apart. Some films that won Academy Awards (or nominations at least) in the early '60s were *The Alamo, Elmer Gantry, Fanny, The Guns of Navarone, Judgment at Nuremberg, West Side Story, To Kill a Mockingbird, Mutiny on the Bounty, How the West Was Won, Dr. Strangelove,* and *My Fair Lady.*

Do you see any trends? Certainly there are similarities in the three generations' movies, but the differences are striking. Consider, for example, depictions of war. The Boomers saw unbridled, unashamed heroism in *The Alamo;* Xers' cynical view of the purposes of war is depicted in *Platoon, Apocalypse Now,* and *The Deer Hunter,* which were much bloodier and more graphic than ever before; and the Millennials look either to the past *(Braveheart)* or to the future *(Independence Day),* but both contain more blood or explosions than ever before. Boomers gloried in triumphant war; Xers lamented purposeless death in war; and Millennials fantasize about the excitement of war.

Like that of television, the pace of movies today is much quicker than in previous eras. Shots often last only a few seconds, and in some cases, several shots take place in a single second. Only a few years ago, we had three networks to choose from. Then local cable channels came on board. Then Fox started its national network, and many more cable networks began. Today with satellite dishes, viewers can channel surf and find hundreds—maybe thousands—of choices.

One of the choices is pornographic movies. Network programming seems to rely on the ratings to shield young viewers from skin, so prime-time programs often depict soft porn scenes. And hard-core pornography is available through almost any cable provider. Too many parents don't screen their children from either soft or hard-core porn. NBC News reported that the production of hard-core pornographic videos has increased almost 700 percent in the '90s. Police are cracking down on child porn, but it seems to me that this is closing the barn door after the cows get out. The normalization of pornography in our culture is alarming.

SEXUAL ACTIVITY

According to a 1997 report by the *Journal of the American Medical Association,* "approximately 17% of 7th and 8th graders and nearly half (49.3%) of 9th through 12th graders indicated that they had ever had sexual intercourse."[2] The teen birth rate decreased slightly in the past few years, but the actual number of births has remained relatively constant at record numbers due to the increased population of teenagers.[3]

In the United States, many of us have become calloused to the news reports of teen pregnancy because we see these reports so often. However, we need to be aware that the birthrate in our country is almost double that of the United Kingdom (60 per 1,000 compared to 32 per 1,000) and fully fifteen times the rate in Japan (4 per 1,000). The abortion rates are similarly disproportionate.[4]

The recent mass advertising campaigns and news reporting about AIDS have been designed to warn people—especially the young—against having unprotected sex. It is true that Millennials are using condoms slightly more than before, but the gains are negligible. *Easy sex* is the term often used to describe the sexual mores of teenagers today, but the risks are greater than ever. Dr. Joe S. McIlhaney Jr. of the Medical Institute for Sexual Health reports that condoms fail to block HIV fully 31 percent of the time. Not good odds for sexual Russian roulette! And AIDS is only the tip of the iceberg.

In *The Hidden Epidemic,* Thomas R. Eng and William T. Butler of the Institute of Medicine report:

> Each year, approximately 3 million American teenagers acquire an STD [sexually transmitted disease]. During the past two decades, sexual intercourse among adolescents has steadily increased, resulting in an enlarging pool of young men and women at risk for STDs . . . Adolescents (10–19 years of age) . . . are the age group at greatest risk for acquiring STD, for a number of reasons: they are more likely to have multiple sex partners; they may be more likely to engage in unprotected intercourse; and their partners may be at higher risk for being infected compared to most adults . . . Female adolescents are also more susceptible to cervical infections, such as gonorrhea and chlamydial infection, because the cervix of female adolescents and young women is especially sensitive to infection by certain sexually transmitted organisms.

They also report that rates of gonorrhea and chlamydia in the general population have decreased in recent years, but the statistics for these diseases among teenagers have actually risen. They conclude, "In some studies, up to 30–40 percent of sexually active adolescent females studied have been infected" with chlamydia.[5]

The high divorce rates in the past twenty years and the concurrent increase in teen sex may have a strong parallel. As fathers have been absent from the home environment, or almost absent because they choose to work seventy to eighty hours a week, they obviously have less time to spend with their children, to nurture, to laugh, to direct. And with the rapid rise of rates of both parents working, children in these families often feel a great need for warmth, love, and attention. Teenagers, especially girls, mistake sex for intimacy. In a survey by *Seventeen* magazine, only 1.1 percent said sex is more important than affection. They long for a loving relationship, but they often settle for sex.[6]

The good news is that several factors have a significant, positive influence on the sexual behavior of teenagers. The *Journal of the American Medical Association (JAMA)* reports that pledges, strong families, high expectations in school, and religion all play a role in delaying the onset of sexual activity.

The True Love Waits campaign has obviously had a profound impact: "Adolescents who reported having taken a pledge to remain a virgin were at significantly lower risk of early age sexual debut. Nearly 16% of females and 10% of males reported making such pledges."[7]

It is not surprising that the *JAMA* notes the instrumental role of family relationships: "Significant family factors associated with delaying sexual debut included high levels of parent-family 'connectedness,' parental disapproval of their adolescent being sexually active, and parental disapproval of their adolescent's using contraception." The last part of the statement makes a loud and clear call against much of the sex ed material in public schools.

But the *JAMA* also provides a sobering statistic about family life today. It cites a study conducted by *Science* magazine: "Compared with 1960, children in the United States have lost, on average, 10 to 12 hours per week of parental time."[8] Parents need to realize their God-given responsibility to nurture, protect, and equip their children to make good choices. Too much is at stake to fail them.

Parents also play a key role in their expectations for their children's school performance. According to the *JAMA* article, three educational factors have an impact on the sexual purity of children: parental involvement with teachers, parent-teacher organizations, and other school activities; attendance at a parochial school where values are taught and modeled openly; and attendance at a school with a high average daily attendance. Academic excellence was noted as somewhat important in delaying sexual involvement, but it did not seem to be nearly as significant as these three factors.

Finally, religion makes a difference in the sexual decisions of young people. Of course, the True Love Waits campaign has a strong Christian value system, so there is some overlap in these factors, but prayer and active involvement in church and youth groups provide a relatively positive peer group where conservative values are promoted and respected.

A girl named Sarah called our radio show. She explained that she had slept with fifteen guys in the past two years. She told me, "I just feel like I'm kind of like lost in life, you know? And I just do, you know, things that God doesn't want me to do. You know, I'm a very unhappy person. I remember when I was a happy person, you know, it's when I had God in my life, but I just feel like He doesn't want me there anymore."

I explained to her about God's forgiveness and about the consequences of her actions. Her heart was tender. I told her, "You want to come back to God, don't you, Sarah?"

She replied, "I do, but I don't know if God can forgive me. You see, I killed a life. It's tearing me up inside, you know, and I don't want to see another person go through what I've gone through. I look at my past, and it's scary."

That night, Sarah confessed her sins and returned to the love of the Father. I prayed for her: "God, I thank You that Sarah has been honest with You and honest with me. She wants a new start tonight. Lord, give her hope. Give her a future. Help her to overcome the shame and the guilt and the terror of her abortion. In Christ's name. Amen."

Then I spoke to her again, "In Isaiah 44:22, God said, 'Sarah, I've swept away your sins like a big cloud. I've removed your sins like a cloud that disappears into the air. Come back to Me because I saved you.' And He has done all that tonight, hasn't He, Sarah?"

This dear young woman knew that her behavior was self-destructive and that it harmed others. She called because she wanted God to change her heart. I really appreciate the young people who have the courage to take steps like that.

DRUG USE

The entry point for young people to use any type of alcohol or drugs is getting younger and younger. Trying alcohol is common today among fifth graders. Ready access in the home is a dominant factor in many cases for both cigarette and alcohol use. In recent years, the tobacco industry has been attacked for promoting smoking among teens. One report revealed a secret tobacco industry memo that cited studies of children as young as five years old! Even with all the warnings on packages and horrifying reports of smoking-related diseases, a study by the Centers for Disease Control shows that the use of tobacco among high school students has risen at an alarming rate from 1991 to 1997, from 27.5 percent to 36.4 percent. Nearly half of male students (48.2 percent) and more than one-third of female students (36 percent) reported using tobacco during the past month. Smoking among black teens, which had declined over many years, almost doubled during that period.[9] Three factors that correlate with smoking are the desire to appear older than peers, low grades, and a job that requires working more than twenty hours per week.[10]

Hollywood seems to want to promote smoking. A study reported in *Tobacco Control,* a journal published by the British Medical Association, stated, "The incidence of smoking in top-grossing movies has increased during the 1990s, and dramatically exceeds real smoking rates." In the first half of the decade, 80 percent of male leads smoked. The report asserted, "Films continue to present the smoker as one who is typically white, male, middle class, successful and attractive, a movie-hero who takes smoking for granted. The use of tobacco in films is increasing and is reinforcing misleading images that present smoking as a widespread and socially desirable activity." During the 1960s, the survey found, tobacco was used once in every five minutes of film. During the '70s and '80s, it dropped to once in every ten to fifteen minutes, but recently the figure has climbed back to once in every three to five minutes. "These portrayals," the study concluded, "may encourage teenagers—the major movie audience—to smoke."[11]

Marijuana use among young people remains about 12.7 percent, with about one-fourth reporting they had ever smoked "weed." The relatively stable percentages are misleading, however, because today's marijuana is about ten times more potent than the pot Boomers smoked thirty years ago. Marijuana is becoming a hard drug.

Alcohol remains the drug of choice in the United States. Binge drinking among college students is at epidemic proportions. Among adolescents, 17.9 percent report drinking more than once a month, and almost 10 percent drink at least one day each week. The same factors that correlate to cigarette smoking (the desire to appear older than peers, low grades, and a job that requires working more than twenty hours per week) are combined with low self-esteem among young drinkers. Among seventh and eighth graders, the fear of sudden death showed up in the *JAMA* study as a factor that encourages them to drink.

The use of hard stuff has likewise stabilized in recent years, though movies such as *Pulp Fiction* and particular styles of some high-fashion models make heroin look particularly appealing among the young. The use of stimulants, depressants, narcotics, and hallucinogens remains relatively constant at incredibly high levels.

So, are recent parental attention and governmental policies having an impact on the Millennials? Yes, I think the stabilization of rates of increase shows they are. But stabilizing these high rates is hardly a sweeping victory! More must be done for our children. Much more.

A young man named Phil called our radio show. He said he'd

been using pot since he was eleven years old. I asked if he was using anything else. He replied, "Acid and mushrooms, anything I can get ahold of. I did some acid and some 'shrooms yesterday and just, I don't know . . . I want to quit, but I like it, and I know it's messing me up and everything, but . . ."

I asked him, "Why do you do it then?"

"I like it. It makes me feel good."

I sensed there was more to the story. I probed, "Phil, what are you trying to cover?"

"Nothing. It's just, I've been in Boys School three times, in Indiana Boys School three times."

I asked him, "What's that?"

He explained, "It's just a jail for juveniles. I was in rehab there. I thought I learned something the first time I was there, but I didn't. Then I thought I learned something the second time, and I didn't . . . and the third time I didn't learn nothing either."

I encouraged him, "Go on."

"It just seems like my drug habit just keeps getting worse and worse and worse because when I first started, I was, you know, I was just smoking a little weed with my cousin. And then it just kept getting worse, and then he wanted me to try some acid. And then, you know, I just tried acid, and then I was just, like every day I'm doing acid and mushrooms and getting high."

I talked to Phil about the real issue: his need for Jesus Christ. I explained that he was trying to fill the hole in his heart with the wrong thing. Only Christ could give him the peace and fulfillment he longed for. After more conversation, Phil opened his heart to the Savior. I hope he is walking with Christ today.

TECHNOLOGY

A chief characteristic of the Millennial Generation is that they are *plugged in.* To Boomers in the early '60s, that term would have meant plugging in the hi-fi. To Xers in the late '70s, it would have meant listening to a cassette tape on a Walkman. Today's Millennials probably don't know what an LP is, and they have long since discarded (or never used) cassette tapes. They use the latest technology for music, television, information, and games. The most dramatic change has been in the development of computers.

I looked up *computer history* on the Web, and I found a wealth of information (as you'd expect). There are on-line museums, research papers, charts, and time lines. Let me give you a quick history of computing during the last three generations:

- 1943: The army bought the ENIAC design from Drs. John Mauchly and Persper Eckert. Their goal was to compute missile trajectory within two days. Construction took 200,000 man-hours, 500,000 soldered joints, 18,000 vacuum tubes, 6,000 switches, and 500 terminals. Output was on punch cards.

- 1953: The UNIVAC was created by Remington Rand under the direction of retired General Leslie R. Groves, who used a two-team, competitive approach to development, much like the Manhattan Project's creation of the atom bomb during World War II. The 409 was the first electromagnetic computer of stand-alone, modular design, which allowed the replacement of parts by modules.

- 1971: Bill Gates and Paul Allen form Traf-O-Data to create and sell traffic analysis systems.

- 1972: Intel introduces the 8008, the first 8-bit microprocessor.

- 1974: Vint Cerf and Bob Kahn publish "A Protocol for Packet Network Internetworking."

- 1975: On the cover of the magazine, *Popular Electronics* features the MITS Altair 8800 as the first "personal computer." It was a kit people could order from the magazine.
  Microsoft is created.

- 1977: Apple sells its Apple II for $1,195, without a monitor.
- 1980: Apple has 50 percent of the personal computer market.

  Microsoft approaches IBM about a personal computer project.
- 1981: The IBM PC is launched.
- 1983: Desktop workstations appear, many using IP networking software.
- 1984: Macintosh is introduced by Apple.

  Number of hosts breaks 1,000.
- 1985: Microsoft Windows 1.0 is introduced.

  Whole Earth 'Lectronic Link (WELL) is established.
- 1987: Number of hosts breaks 10,000.

  Microsoft sales top $1 billion.

  Number of hosts breaks 100,000.
- 1992: Number of hosts breaks 1,000,000.
- 1993: Web grows at 341,634 percent annual rate.
- 1994: Net traffic passes 10 trillion bytes per month.
- 1998: Thirty-six percent of net surfers have been on-line for less than a year.

  Net commerce is up 20 percent in the past six months.

  Apple, which has lost much of its market share, introduces the iMac G3.[12]

Software is being introduced at an incredible pace. Most of this, of course, is driven by business, but Millennials are enjoying the benefits of riding on business's coattails. They use computers to do homework, to stay in touch with friends through E-mail, to chat with strangers, and to play the newest games. (More on all this in a later chapter.)

The difference between Millennials today and Xers in the mid-'70s is almost the same as between Millennials and Boomers in their youth. Neither Xers nor Boomers had access to personal computers until they were introduced in 1977. Even then, the first PCs were available only in kits, so they had to be assembled by someone who really knew what he was doing. It would be years until the majority of Xers had access to PCs, and when they did, they loved them! Some Boomers recall being at universities that had computers. One man was a student at Georgia Tech in the late '60s. He remembers his friends who took computer courses carrying boxes of punch cards over to the computer lab to run a program. Every card (and there were often thousands) had to be punched perfectly, or the computer would lock up or spit out useless cards for hours!

The proliferation of pornography on the Web is a great concern to parents. Years ago, boys had to go to the store and get an older brother or a stranger to buy a copy of *Playboy* for them. And when they got it home, there was always the threat of its being found by parents, no matter how carefully they hid it. Often, it just wasn't worth the trouble. Today, however, boys can have the full array of hard pornography on-line any time. The social purchasing inhibitions have been taken away.

EDUCATION

Assistant high school principal Kristi LaMell noted the trends in education in the past generation. Starting in the middle to late '70s, many states saw the need for competency testing to stop the social promotions and graduations of students who could not read or write. Today, a majority of states require students to pass tests of basic skills in order to be promoted and to graduate from high school. In the '70s, LaMell maintained, students studied more than current students do, but the body of available knowledge was far less expansive than that available today. High school students now have the world at their fingertips through the Internet, and they have far more information because they can easily acquire it. Television news also contributes to the explosion of students' knowledge. Students twenty years ago had to read the newspaper to learn about events in the world, and few students were motivated to read the papers. Today, they only need to flip the channel to CNN or other news broadcasts to instantly see events as they unfold across the globe.

LaMell's other observations about education's shifts in the past couple of decades include the following:

- Twenty years ago, special ed students were segregated from other kids. Today, they are a part of the culture of the high school in the "least restrictive environment."

- Twenty years ago, students received more parental supervision and encouragement than today, and there were far fewer distractions for the average student. The decline in parental involvement and the increase in distractions for today's students have led to a larger gap between top students (who receive that encouragement and shielding from distractions) and the bottom (who don't).

- Twenty years ago, high school was the center of students' social lives. Dances, sports, proms, and most other gatherings happened at the school or under the school's sponsorship. Today, most students focus their social activities away from school at malls and other off-campus hangouts.

- Twenty years ago, students were relatively naive about drugs, premarital sex, profanity, and other vices. These have become normalized for today's young people. They are worldly and blasé in their approach to these issues.

- Twenty years ago, students were very safe on campus. Throwing spit wads was one of teachers' most significant complaints. Today, almost every high school has police on campus to guard the lives of students and teachers.

To make her point, LaMell told about an event that took place twenty years ago. One spring day, a group of guys forged a note to get out of their last-period class so they could see their buddies play an out-of-town baseball game. When they were caught, the students received severe discipline for the breach of school conduct. Today, forging notes and skipping classes for no good reason (not to support other students) are such a typical part of life at school that the significance pales in comparison to the far bigger issues on campus, such as weapons and drugs.

I asked LaMell what she predicted high schools would be like twenty years from now. She said that if the problems escalate in the next two decades as they have in the past twenty years, there won't be compulsory attendance beyond the middle school level. Only students who want to learn will come to school. The others will enter trade schools or the job market. Does this sound extreme? Not any more extreme than what has happened in the past two decades.

TWENTY FACTS

The Children's Defense Fund publishes its own window on the status of our culture: *20 Key Facts About American Children.* They let us see some of the needs that often go unnoticed. These are the stats about Millennial kids:

1. 1 in 2 preschoolers has a mother in the labor force.

2. 1 in 2 will live with a single parent at some point in childhood.

3. 1 in 2 never completes a single year of college.

4. 1 in 3 is born to unmarried parents.

5. 1 in 4 is born poor.

6. 1 in 4 is born to a mother who did not graduate from high school.

7. 1 in 5 is born to a mother who did not receive prenatal care in the first three months of pregnancy.

8. 1 in 5 lives in a family receiving food stamps.

9. 1 in 5 is poor today.

10. 1 in 6 has a foreign-born mother.

11. 1 in 7 has no health insurance.

12. 1 in 7 has a worker in the family but still is poor.

13. 1 in 8 is born to a teen mother.

14. 1 in 8 never graduates from high school.

15. 1 in 9 is born into a family living at less than half the poverty level ($6079 for a family of three).

16. 1 in 12 has a disability.

17. 1 in 14 was born at low birthweight.

18. 1 in 21 is born to a mother who received late or no pre-natal care.

19. 1 in 25 lives with neither parent.

20. 1 in 610 will be killed by a gun before age 20.[13]

So What?

I hope this quick tour of our pop culture through the last few decades was enlightening—and even fun!—for you. Did I leave out your favorite movie, singing group, or television program? I hope not. The point is this: developmental factors remain constant in youth culture from one generation to the next, but the forces of our culture are driving families apart, promoting sex and drugs, and undermining the foundation of truth. The images and sounds of the past thirty to forty years give us a loud and clear message. Sure, the steep increases in drug use and sex during the Xers' youth have been arrested. That's great. But we aren't gaining any ground we've lost. And in the field of morals and truth, we're losing even more ground. The culture is speaking to us. We'd better listen!

4

Eroded Trust

Trust can be measured by the level of expectations: of a child for a parent, of an employer for an employee, of spouses for each other, in a generation of young people for their elders. By most accounts, Millennials do not trust those who claim to lead them and shape their lives. Consider these examples:

- Millennials believe their lives will have more problems and fewer opportunities than their parents had (they are the first generation to believe that).
- They have a poor sense of right and wrong, so they don't highly value the directives of authority figures. They value their own opinions more highly than others'.
- They don't believe politics and government can do anything for them, so they aren't interested in getting involved.
- Their parents belong to a different generation and a different (Enlightenment) way of thinking. The normal separation between adolescents and parents is much wider than usual. Millennials feel even less understood.
- They grope to find heroes to emulate. They find very few.
- No causes grip their hearts and propel them to trust one another to accomplish great goals.

During the part of the historical cycle known as the "unraveling," public trust in civic institutions wanes because they appear to be ineffective in solving the problems of society. The fabric of society is seen to be coming apart at the seams, hence the label: unraveling. According to Strauss and Howe, the current unraveling began in the middle of the Reagan presidency and will last another five to ten years until the next crisis. One of the primary characteristics of Millennials, and perhaps *the* primary characteristic, is that they don't trust authority.

This slide to distrust didn't appear overnight. It has its roots in the rebellion of the Boomers in the late '60s. Boomers rebelled against their parents, who by all accounts were valiant men and women who endured the hardships of the depression and courageously fought—and won—the most extensive war in world history. The Boomers' parents were genuine heroes, but the Boomers picked up on the chaos and uncertainty of the cold war, the civil rights movement, and later, the quagmire in Vietnam. They abhorred the status quo, and they "let it all hang out" in self-fulfillment through lots of drugs and free sex. When these rebellious kids became adults and had families, they became responsible businessmen and businesswomen, but they didn't become good parents.

Xer children grew up in homes in which parents weren't as involved with their kids as they needed to be. Children were, as we have already seen, latchkey kids by the millions. Psychology—and common sense—tells us that parental neglect breeds distrust and insecurity in children. Xers felt and continue to feel that way. The slide toward relativism took hold in that generation. In *The Invisible Generation,* George Barna records, "70% [of Xers] claim that absolute does not exist, that all truth is relative and personal . . . Two thirds of the [Xer] generation concede that 'nothing can be known for certain except the things that you experience in your own life.'"[1]

For the Millennials, times have changed somewhat. Their parents are far more involved than the parents of Xers were, and government has bent over backward to give attention, dollars, and assorted programs for today's kids. But the statistics we saw in the previous chapters tell us that things are really not better. Not much worse, perhaps, but no better. The good intentions of the Decade of the Child have been counterbalanced by the continued erosion of absolutes, the lack of a defining purpose, and fallen role models.

EROSION OF ABSOLUTES

Tolerance seems to be a good thing, so kind, so inclusive, so nonjudgmental. But it comes at a great cost: truth. Human beings have a God-given need for truth and justice. When everything is equally valid, then nothing is really true. Everywhere kids turn, it seems, they are told, "If it's right for you, then it's right," or "Don't judge someone just because he is different." And if a teenager has the gall to talk about biblical truth, he may hear, "How can you be so sure? There's no way you can prove God. Surely God is big enough to include everybody who is sincere." When objective truth is discarded, we are left with the mushy concept of "the truth that is within you." But again, that "truth" is valid only because a person feels it and is sincere, not because it is derived from an external, verifiable source. We will examine this characteristic of Millennials in more depth in a later chapter, but for now, we can say that the rise of relativism has contributed to the erosion of our young people's willingness and capacity to trust authority.

LACK OF A DEFINING PURPOSE

When people have a clear purpose, they are compelled to define who is for them and who is against them. This process forces people to identify friends and enemies and, in doing so, galvanizes relationships, promotes camaraderie, and establishes trust. Millennials have no clear purpose. Their lack of trust is both a product of that fact and a reinforcement of it. Let's see how we got here.

The Boomers' parents had to go to war or stay behind and work in factories to support the war effort to stop world domination by the dictators in Germany, Italy, and Japan. They were galvanized with a clear, strong goal. They didn't have to wonder what great cause they could give their lives for.

The Boomers, too, grew up when right and wrong were identifiable. "The Soviet menace" wasn't an empty threat. Hundreds of intercontinental ballistic missiles were pointed at our cities. And for a few terrifying days in October 1962, President Kennedy and the nation stared nuclear war in the face when we found Soviet missiles on launch pads in Cuba, just ninety miles from American soil.

Every person had to consider and decide how to respond to integration. Many whites despised Martin Luther King's attempts to win equal rights for blacks until younger, discontented blacks such as H. Rap Brown and Stokely Carmichael took the leadership of the movement and King's nonviolence gave way to urban riots, burning, and death.

The space race was kicked into high gear when John Kennedy pledged to "put a man on the moon and bring him back before the end of this decade." Incredible resources were harnessed in our country to accomplish that goal.

Our country pledged to stop the "dominoes" of countries from falling to the Communists, and we drew the line in the sand in South Vietnam. Soon, however, pride in our military disintegrated into confusion, then anger at a war without fronts, against an enemy we couldn't identify, for a purpose we didn't believe in. Americans took sides. Boomers had purpose. In fact, they had several compelling ones to choose from!

In 1969, Neil Armstrong set foot on the moon. President Nixon negotiated détente with the Soviets. Schools, government facilities, restaurants, public transportation, and virtually every aspect of American life became integrated—grudgingly perhaps, but integrated anyway. Then came the bitter end of the Vietnam

War and the scandal of Watergate. Confidence in our nation's sense of purpose waned. Distrust settled in. A peanut farmer from Georgia became president, the economy took a nosedive, interest rates hit 21 percent, and a renegade band of zealots in Iran kidnapped our embassy staff and held them hostage for 444 days. And we couldn't do anything about it.

The Reagan, Bush, and Clinton years have witnessed unprecedented economic prosperity, but we have not experienced any challenge that has given our young people something to live and die for. Recently I asked students to identify the causes of their generation, and blank expressions were their answers. I told them about the country's commitments during World War II, the cold war, civil rights, the space race, and even the polarization during the Vietnam era. Their eyes lit up, then one of them said sadly, "We don't have anything like that."

Arguably the most compelling issue of our day is global warming, but it is hardly a nail-biter. A recent Gallup poll found that only 34 percent of Americans would be willing to risk any change in their standard of living to take steps to reduce the greenhouse effect. The percentage of the public concerned about the problem has actually declined since a 1991 poll was taken, and more than half (58 percent) think the United States shouldn't sign a treaty that grants exceptions to any large nations such as Russia and Brazil. Beyond this, there are considerable confusion and debate among the general population about whether global warming even exists.[2]

Somehow, global warming just doesn't do it as a gripping cause to live and die for.

FALLEN ROLE MODELS

First, you have to have heroes. Then you follow them. A sense of stability is undermined in a generation without people to look up to. Trust is violated, and they wander around looking for someone to believe in.

Think of the Boomers in their adolescence. Who were the heroes then? Audie Murphy was the most decorated soldier in World War II. He made (seemingly) dozens of movies about heroic combat exploits. Dozens of other combat veterans risked all or gave all. Stories abounded about those men and women as a grateful nation basked in victory. Only a little later, young John Kennedy took the reins at the White House and brought in "the best and the brightest" young men and women to run the country. For many Boomers, their heroes were people in government. (Can you believe that? If you are old enough, you can remember those bygone days.) Martin Luther King and Andrew Young, Alan Shepard and John Glenn, the rest of the original astronauts who had "the right stuff," and countless other lesser lights showed us what dedication and valor were about in the Boomer years of youth.

Times changed. The bloom fell off, and antiheroes captured the headlines. Tom Hayden and Jane Fonda led protests. H. Rap Brown and Malcolm X spoke for their people. Allen Ginsberg wrote poetry—which millions of young people actually read—about discontent, homosexuality, drugs, and being an outcast. And the protests spilled over into sports when John Carlos and Tommy Smith bowed their heads and raised clenched fists in a Black Power salute on the medal platform in the 1972 Olympic Summer Games.

The era of economic prosperity and the absence of challenge or intense purpose in our country have left us with few real heroes. In politics, President Clinton has been accused of having oral sex with a White House intern and lying about his business dealings in Arkansas when he was governor and asking an Arkansas state employee for sex and having a mistress for twelve years and lying repeatedly to cover up his behavior. Pulitzer prize–winning syndicated columnist Paul Greenberg compared the proliferation of excuses coming out of the Clinton White House with Nixon's Watergate fiasco. Greenberg concluded, "Compared to this president

[Clinton], Nixon was a bungling amateur at excuses, denials, explanations, memory loss, indignant statements, pained silences, television presence, lip-chewing sincerity and general huffery-puffery."[3] The net result, Greenberg asserted, is that Americans' expectations of our national leader spiral downward:

> By now the president of the United States has become a figure to deride or defend in American society rather than a role model. The result is that American standards in general decline with every new Clinton scandal and the ever stranger explanations thereof. The bizarre has become the routine . . . Conduct once considered abhorrent may be thought of as the norm once higher standards have been eroded.

And the majority of the American public don't seem to care as long as the economy continues to roll along.

Astronauts? Sure, we still have them taking the shuttles up every few months, but who can name the crews? War heroes? We fought for a few days in Grenada and Panama in the '80s, and we fought in Iraq's Desert Storm in 1991, but besides General Norman Schwarzkopf, can any of us name a hero of these brief conflicts?

I asked those same students to name their heroes. They instantly mentioned a raft of athletes and Hollywood celebrities. Have these people done anything truly heroic? No, but they're the best we can offer this generation. Tiger Woods was mentioned several times, but so was Dennis Rodman. There seems to be very little capacity to differentiate between "good guys" and "bad guys." Celebrity is enough.

In late 1997, Latrell Sprewell of the NBA's Golden State Warriors got fed up with his coach, P. J. Carlesimo. After a stormy practice session shouting match, Sprewell left the court and went to take a shower. He returned about twenty minutes later, grabbed Carlesimo by the throat, choked him, and threatened to kill him. The Warriors suspended Sprewell, and the National Basketball

Association levied its longest nondrug-related suspension ever: one year. An arbitrator, however, reduced the suspension to seven months and ordered the Warriors to reinstate Sprewell to the team—along with the $17 million left on his contract.

On a *60 Minutes* exposé about Sprewell, reporter Leslie Stahl walked with Sprewell to an outdoor court in Sacramento. A flock of kids rushed up to them and asked Sprewell for his autograph. One of the boys said, "Hey, you really kicked your coach's butt!" He is a hero to the Millennials.

The most popular face in America today is Michael Jordan. He is, by most evaluations, the greatest basketball player ever to play the game. In an article for *Sky* magazine, Jonathan Yardley contrasts the heroes of the Boomer generation, specifically Dwight Eisenhower, with today's top hero:

> To say that the transition from Ike to Mike is a transition from hero to celebrity is an oversimplification, but not much of one. Ours is a culture—one we are rapidly exporting to the rest of the world—that honors mere fame far more than it does hard achievement. The struggles of our formative years, struggles that produced such indisputable heroes as George Washington, Abraham Lincoln and Harriet Tubman, are no longer being fought. We are a mature democracy, an imperfect one to be sure, but one rarely placed at risk in circumstances from which heroes emerge. Yet we still want and need heroes, as every society does, so we have redefined the term.[4]

Yardley observes that our nation is fabulously wealthy by world and historic standards, and we are not preoccupied with survival, national defense, or rampant disease. We have so much affluence that we can afford to be distracted by entertainment. Michael Jordan, he asserts, is not a hero in the classic sense of the word. He hasn't rescued any lives or achieved death-defying deeds. But in our culture, *hero* has to be redefined to "taking command of difficult situations and obtaining victory through sheer will." And Michael Jordan, Yardley says, embodies this definition.

He laments,

> There is much in this country which troubles me. I worry that the entertainment culture may be shoving aside the work ethic, that we prefer fantasy and "docudrama" and "infotainment" to cold reality and rigorous education, that self-discipline is giving way to self-indulgence, that the great struggles in which we once united have left in their wake petty squabbles that divide. I worry, too, that we admire, even venerate, too many people who do not deserve it."

But Michael Jordan, he asserts, deserves it.

I thank God that we don't face worldwide calamity today. I am thankful that we are free to pursue our dreams and speak our minds. And I am grateful for all our material blessings in this great country. I only wish we had more heroic heroes.

The distrust of Millennials takes several forms. Many of them absorb the relativism and purposelessness of our society and become passive. They sit back and watch the world go by, focusing only on their small realm of friends and interests. They aren't hopeless; they're disengaged. Some, however, sense the emptiness around them and are angry about it. They are determined to get to the top of something. Their energies could be channeled into worthwhile causes, but they can't find any. Some of them pour themselves into making money, some into sports (which has become increasingly violent and competitive at all levels), and some just fight anybody who challenges them. Another kind of young person feels insecure, but refuses to admit it. The feeling is simply too threatening, so they assure themselves that somebody somewhere is trustworthy. And maybe they will find that person someday.

Distrust leads naturally to skepticism about anybody who

gives them quick, simple answers—and in this relativistic culture, any answers at all! They have a world of information, but they are confused about what really matters. They won't listen to those who would give them direction because Millennials don't trust these adults or teachers. And they even don't trust many of their peers, so they split off into smaller groups for comfort and security.

I believe this lack of trust is the central, defining issue of the Millennial Generation. It isn't the most visible, but it shapes all the others.

5

Information Without Wisdom

We recently did a radio show on Marilyn Manson, and one of the guys who works with us, Bill Scott, went to a chat room after the show. I sat in and we told the kids I was coming on-line. I was amazed at the power and the passion that came across the screen, and how much empathy and emotion the young people shared on the chat line. Some said, "We're behind you all the way, Dawson. Make your stand against Marilyn Manson!" Others said, "How could you be so judgmental about Marilyn Manson?" A few encouraged us: "Are you holding up okay under the pressure of doing a show on Marilyn Manson? We're praying for you!" But others said, "What are you talking about? Who's Dawson McAllister, anyway?" I was amazed at the honesty, passion, and power of those messages on the chat line. Internet communication is a whole new way of communicating—for good or for bad. It is beyond anything I have ever seen before.

A recent report states that more than ten million children accessed the Internet in the past year. That figure is double from the previous year, which was double the year before that. The Internet and Millennials: astronomical growth!

Pollster and social analyst George Barna has noted that young people today are caught in a vise: they quickly make decisions, yet they spend little time with adults who might provide wisdom and direction. The art of reflection is lost on most Millennials. They have become used to rapid-fire media images, instant access to the Internet, fast food, and speed in almost every other area of their lives. They have an incredibly vast array of knowledge available to them on the Web, all day every day. And they use it. Decision making has become almost spontaneous. In addition, the average child today spends ten to twelve fewer hours per week relating to his parents than did the average child one generation ago. This combination provides plenty of information, but very little wisdom.

Think about this for a minute. For hundreds of generations, children had few amusements or distractions. They spent most of their time working alongside their parents, siblings, and extended family on farms or in shops. There was plenty of time to ponder, reflect, and consider—and far less information for them to process. The industrial revolution changed that for millions of individuals and families as many moved from farms to factories. Time with family members was relegated to the hours after work (which often was ten to twelve hours a day, six days a week). From the mid-1700s until the 1960s, farm populations dwindled as people moved in droves to urban areas. Their diversions were family games, books, church, and later radio.

In the '60s, however, the technology revolution began to take shape. Suddenly computers, televisions, and advanced machines of all kinds promised to make life easier in homes, businesses, and factories. The knowledge needed for this advanced technology increased exponentially, along with advances in medicine and virtually every other field. For the first time, families at home turned toward something besides one another: the television. They didn't talk to one another much because somebody on the tube was talking to them. Information was increasing, but quality family time was decreasing.

The knowledge explosion became thermonuclear in the '80s in

the information revolution. When computers came to homes in significant numbers, and then when the Internet's use spread widely, the average person suddenly had access to more information than anyone ever dreamed possible only a few years before. Cable television brought dozens of additional channels into living rooms. Advanced computers linked people with information at astonishing speed (astonishing at least until the next computer came out). The increase in divorce rates, vast media options, the incredibly busy pace of life brought on by machines that supposedly make life more convenient—all these things have taken time away from parents and children. They have less time to talk and reflect together, and they spend the time they have racing to the next event or arguing about who gets to use the technology tonight.

I'm not trying to start a new chapter of the Luddites (a group named for Ned Ludd in England; in the early nineteenth century, they were against the spread of technology when it was relatively tame, and they smashed machinery in a crusade to stop the steady progress of the industrial revolution), but I want to show how we have come to this point in our culture's history. The link between the proliferation of information and our children's lack of reflection is strong. Their lack of wisdom correlates with the fewer meaningful hours they spend with their parents. Information is not a bad thing at all. The absence of wisdom is, however, sad and dangerous.

Xers learned to use computer technology. Millennials grew up immersed in it. They take it for granted. One boy summed up the experience of countless others. He was five years old when his brothers began using a computer for their homework. He watched them for a while, then, "I just started playing games. I found a whole bunch of stuff that interested me, and I just got hooked on it."[1]

Sixty-four percent of schools have Internet access, and many school libraries offer after-school Internet groups. The use of the Web in public education is expected to continue to grow rapidly as our culture becomes increasingly dependent on information technology.

The impact of this explosion of information, and our children's preoccupation with it, has deep and broad effects, which we'll briefly discuss here.

EXPOSURE TO OPTIONS

They can pull up more than one million Web sites on almost any and every imaginable topic: philosophies, religions, lifestyle choices, to name a few. But without the filter of wisdom, they may see all of these as equally valid. Just as the print media seemed to legitimize any perspective as "truth" in years past, the fact that something is on the Web legitimizes it to unwary surfers.

CHAT LINE CHAOS

Some kids say chat lines are boring, but many get hooked on the idea of saying anything they want to somebody they can't see. Harmless fun? Most of the time, but occasionally danger lurks in the shadows. Chat lines are places where kids can share their feelings, hopes, fears, and ignorance. In one way, they are very safe because the two are not face-to-face, but the free-ranging anonymity can be dangerous. An investigator for Houston Police Department's Computer Crime/Forensic Unit (a computer crime police unit? and you still think times haven't changed?) stated, "In a chat room, you can take on any identity you want. If your kid is interested in the Internet, look over his shoulder, see what he's writing."[2] A naive child can be entranced and duped by a shrewd kid (or adult).

ON-LINE FUN AND GAMES

I asked a group of high school students to identify games they play on the Web or on CD-ROMs. They quickly listed *Myst, Riven,*

Diablo, Warcraft, Doom, Duke Nukem, and *Unreal,* among others. Do you remember the stern warning a few years ago about the game *Dungeons and Dragons*? Those same warnings could be sounded for many of today's games, but we hear few people expressing concern. Some of the games, of course, are harmless fun, but as the movies become more sexual and violent, we can only expect interactive games to follow suit. Many of these are not Super Mario Brothers! A study done by the Recreational Software Advisory Council of Cambridge, Massachusetts, found 46 percent contained violence, and 28 percent of them received a Violence #2 rating or above, which indicates humans being killed or injured. Twenty percent warranted a special rating for blood and gore. Solitaire and computer golf these ain't!

Violence is not the only concern. Several years ago, a University of Miami study of the top-rated games showed that almost nine out of ten excluded women from any leading roles. Male figures dominated by a 13 to 1 ratio. Perhaps worse, almost one-third of the games depicted women as helpless victims who had been kidnapped and needed to be rescued by men.

Recently I talked to a youth pastor who told me one of his kids was spending $250 a month on computer video games. The youth pastor asked him about it, and he said, "When I play video games, the people on the other side can't really hurt me. I am safe playing these games." That was a profound answer. This kid and many like him think the people on the other side of the video games can't hurt them. They fail to understand that they are being hurt in two ways. Number one, they are being pulled away from meaningful one-on-one relationships that would help them develop emotionally. And number two, they are learning the lie that violence has no consequences.

Sometimes I wonder whether some of the recent killings in high schools were the results of normalized and sanitized violence. Did they think the kids and teachers they shot would get up and go on with life when the "game" was over? Or did they realize the blood and the funerals were really real? Did they think somehow they would flip a switch and everything would be okay? The pervasive violence in movies, television, and especially interactive video games has a numbing effect. They think you can shoot a bunch of people, turn off the screen, and go out for pizza. But their minds and perceptions have been terribly wounded by these games. So on the one hand, they feel it's safe, but on the other hand, they are really doing damage. One of the primary uses of chat lines is for the dissemination of information about the newest and most exciting game to be found and downloaded from the Web.

DANGEROUS INFORMATION

For years, we have heard about people finding the designs for bombs on the Internet. There are more of these today. You can search the Web and find plans to make almost any type of incendiary device imaginable, from simple pipe bombs (such as the one used at the Atlanta Olympic Games) to nuclear devices.

SMUT

Parents are understandably outraged about the ease with which their children can access pornography. And it seems to be everywhere! For instance, a friend was doing some research about teenagers, so he entered *teenager* into a popular search engine. The search found tens of thousands of sites. He began scrolling through the listing and soon was in the middle of scores of listings of teen pornography with the most graphic descriptions he had ever seen. You don't have to look for pornography to find it. Our Hope Line fielded 65,000 calls last year; 1,500 of them were from young people struggling with pornography, and since pornography is one of the most secretive of problems, I would guess the problem is far deeper and wider than that figure suggests.

Not long ago, the Mars mission drew the attention of millions of adults and schoolchildren. When many of them tried to access NASA, they typed in a URL (Uniform Resource Locator) NASA.com instead of the official Web site, NASA.gov, which contained all the information about the mission to Mars. When they made the mistake, they saw a banner pornography site and direct links to hard-core sex pictures.

Some of the new technology allows advertisers to "push" links to their sites to E-mail addresses, including yours. An unsuspecting person, such as a child, may open his E-mail and find direct access to a pornographic site.

Psychologically the Web makes it difficult for children, especially adolescent boys, to avoid temptation. When an unwary user clicks on some innocuous intro pages, the splash screen rolls over unless the person intentionally stops it. Graphic porn can surprise a surfer unless he deliberately says no to stop the link and go somewhere else. The necessity to say no to temptation is simply too much for many young surfers. They succumb, are titillated, and easily get hooked, especially if no one is monitoring their use of the Internet.

IMPATIENCE

It is amazing, truly amazing, what power and creativity capitalism employs! The pace of the introduction of generations of new computer technology is growing so rapidly, their advent can be compared to labor pains. Advertising touts each new entry as the latest and greatest, and the ones it replaces as old, slow, and antiquated. Pentium II, G3, and who knows what is next. (It's silly to include the names of any software because these, too, will be outdated by the time the book is a few months old!) And speed is the name of the game. Computers only a few years old are like tortoises (dead ones) compared to the new versions. As if the new technology isn't amazingly fast enough, a consortium of Internet providers is planning on introducing a new system that will make Net access thirty times faster!

Planned obsolescence. Built-in discontent. The advertising and competition make users, young and old, dissatisfied and impatient with anything but the latest, best, and fastest on the market. We've talked about instant gratification in the past, but this is the real thing. It has to be *now!* And all this translates into less reflection, quicker decision making, and more fascination with technology so they spend less time with mature, responsible people and even less wisdom in decision making.

ISOLATION

There is certainly nothing wrong with being fascinated with the incredible technology on the market today. And it's not only speed. Recent developments in graphics software make it possible for the average Joe (with a computer with adequate memory and a few bucks) to create special effects only Steven Spielberg could produce a few years ago. Too often, though, fascination draws the child deeper and deeper into the world of "the square-headed girlfriend" and away from interaction with real people. No, it's not a problem for a kid to spend time playing a game or trying out new graphics software, but if this becomes an obsession (and the makers of games and software clearly want people to oooh and ahhh over them), it could be a major problem for the child. Normal, healthy development requires lots of interaction between a child and his parents, siblings, and peers. When this development is stifled, we all suffer.

Most kids are way beyond their parents in the ability to utilize today's technology. Advertisements show children using the latest software, then turning to the camera, smiling, and saying, "It's so easy, even Dad can use it!" There is nothing wrong with being old-fashioned, with not being on top of today's software and new computers, unless you want to relate to today's kids. It's in their blood. If we want to understand them so that we are effective parents and ministers, we need to "walk a mile in their shoes," which today would be translated, "surf the net an hour or so."

6

Truth? Who Cares?

Millennials do. It's their source of truth that's the problem, not their desire to find truth. As we have seen, many of them don't trust authorities such as parents, government, or church to give them answers. The postmodern, post-Christian slide away from reason and propositional truth has undercut any foundations. The mass of available information and the speed of decision making make careful reflection passé. What are they left with? Personal experience. That's what really matters, that's what they value above all else, and that's what they seek.

A GLIMPSE INTO THE CULTURE

If you haven't seen the movie *Contact*, I recommend that you take some time to watch it. (It's on video by now, so it won't cost you much.) This film will give you a glimpse of how both Xers and Millennials view truth. In the movie, the brilliant, young, beautiful astronomer Ellie Arroway (played by Jodie Foster) has spent her life in the passionate pursuit of a signal from extraterrestrials. She has met the handsome young Palmer Joss (played by Matthew McConaughey) who studied to be a priest, but left the ministry because he "couldn't cut the celibacy thing." After years of painstaking, yet fruitless pursuit, Ellie makes contact with alien beings in the Vega galaxy. The scientists decipher a complex code sent by the beings, and an incredible transport is built to send someone to meet them. Ellie wants desperately to be the person chosen to go, but she is bypassed—and heartbroken.

During these years, Palmer becomes, on his own, a national celebrity who warns against the evils of technological hubris. He and Ellie become reacquainted, and they have deep conversations about the existence of God and the meaning of life. Ellie, the essence of the skeptical scientist who must have empirical evidence to believe, is not swayed by Palmer's faith in God. Now, as the transport construction reaches completion, Palmer is interviewed by Larry King, and he tells the viewing audience, "We've made tremendous advances in technology. We can communicate with each other more quickly and in more ways than ever before . . . but we are more lonely than ever." He is the voice of wisdom. (Maybe he would have been a Luddite!)

The role of Christians constitutes a significant subplot in the movie. When the public finds out about the contact with extraterrestrials, thousands come to the desert observatory where Ellie works. Some came to watch, but the Christians are conspicuous in their shallow, anachronistic reaction against progress and against contacts with the beings. Many Christians foretell the end of the world if somebody converses with these E.T.s. One believer, however, stands in center stage. A fiery, wild-eyed young evangelist with long white stringy hair (and he has bad teeth too!) stands on his platform as Ellie drives slowly by. He points his bony finger (what else?) at her and accuses her of sending the human race into ruin and abandoning God. We see this unsavory guy again just as the transport is ready to be used. He is strapped with explosives. As a suicide bomber, he blows up the device, the hardworking scientists and, it seems, the hope of touching intelligent life in the heavens.

Ahhh, but a second transport was secretly built in a remote location in Japan. The hope is still alive. Ellie is now chosen to be the person to enter the capsule, fly through time, and contact the alien race. Her journey is a jolting, beautiful, touching embrace of the unknown. She returns in wide-eyed wonder at what she saw and felt. But there is one little problem: all the indicators at mission control say she never left earth. Her report of the fantastic eighteen-hour journey and her experience talking with the extraterrestrials is said to be a fraud. A national court of inquiry is convened, and in a Joe McCarthy–type hearing, government officials and scientists grill Ellie as hundreds look on in person and millions by television. The inquisitors accuse Ellie of fabricating the whole story. Tension mounts. The climax nears. The camera closes in on the beleaguered scientist, who tells them, "I know what I experienced, and nobody can ever take that away from me." She found her truth.

There are four messages of this movie:

1. Experience is the ultimate measure of meaning.

2. Evangelical, Bible-believing Christians are antiprogress, reactionary, stupid, and dangerous.

3. God's real representative is one who loves passionately, is reasonable and compassionate, but doesn't draw any harsh lines of truth in the sand.

4. Though an experience may be attacked by others (either agnostics or Christians), it is the foundation for personal truth and cannot be dismissed.

See this movie. It is a marvelous window on our culture.

THE CREEP OF RELATIVISM

Relativism is not a recent guest on the public scene. Its encroachment has been slow and steady for hundreds of years, but the pace at which it has enveloped our hearts and minds has sped up considerably in the past couple of decades. One of the first widely read books on this subject was Allan Bloom's *The Closing of the American Mind,* published in 1987. Bloom focused on education and showed how relativism has adversely affected the learning processes in our public schools and universities. George Barna conducted extensive research in the early '90s and published his results in the books *The Frog in the Kettle, The Invisible Generation,* and *Baby Busters: The Disillusioned Generation.* Josh McDowell took Barna's research, expanded it, and applied it in his excellent book *Right from Wrong.*

Nevertheless, some people just don't see what these writers are talking about. They say, "Things are no different now from when I was young. Kids are kids." Perhaps these skeptics are involved with parochial or Christian schools where biblical values are taught all day every day and the effects of media are somehow negated. Perhaps they live in a conservative enclave or community where they are protected from cultural influences. Or perhaps the reality of the crumbling foundations of our society is too much to accept, so they combat the fear with denial: "I can't stand it, so it's not happening." It takes courage to look at our culture and face the facts of the erosion of its bedrock beliefs. Maybe it takes even more courage to look at your child and wonder what he really values when all the Christian jargon is stripped away and core beliefs are exposed.

As a youth worker, I am tremendously frustrated when students tell me, "The truth for you is true, and the truth for me is true, but they may be different truths." This kind of thinking (or lack of thinking) undercuts the power of propositional truth. I tell these students, "On a clear day, either the sky is blue or it isn't. You're talking nonsense to me. Just look outside. The sky is blue. It's not green or pink or polka-dot. It's always blue."

We have to live with certain assumptions as being true. We have to believe it is true that if you jump out of the Empire State Building, the law of gravity will take effect. It is absurd to say, "Well, it may be true for you, but not for me." Even if you don't think it's true, you're going to pay the consequences. Gently and lovingly I say to students who speak to me in this manner that they're playing head games. They have been told that they can make up their own reality, and that reality is valid. Francis Schaeffer used to call biblical truth "true truth." If it isn't, our message is simply dismissed as one more idea in a world of millions of others.

No Golden Age

We may be tempted to look back to some day and age when biblical truth was the centerpiece of life. The Reformation attempted to accomplish that, and it achieved remarkable success studded with remarkable failures such as Luther's participation in the nobles' vicious attacks on common people during the Peasants' Revolt in Germany. Francis Schaeffer wrote,

> There is no golden age in the past which we can idealize—whether it is early America, the Reformation, or the early church. But until recent decades something did exist which can rightly be called a Christian consensus or those which gave a distinctive shape to Western society and to the United States in a definite way. Now that consensus is all but gone, and the freedoms that it brought are being destroyed before our eyes. We are at a time when humanism is coming to its natural conclusion in morals, in values, and in law. All that society has today are relativistic values based upon statistical averages, or the arbitrary decisions of those who hold legal and political power.[1]

Schaeffer was a leading spokesman for the Christian cause against abortion. He and then Surgeon General Dr. C. Everett Koop wrote *Whatever Happened to the Human Race?* to show how abortion became acceptable in America, what effects abortion policy has had on our society, and what believers can do to combat the policy. In the book, they talk about Nazi Germany's use of euthanasia to get rid of "undesirables" in that country. Schaeffer and Koop warn against any dabbling in euthanasia in our country because the slope is too slippery. It can go far in a short amount of time. Schaeffer died a few years ago before the news of Dr. Jack Kevorkian's doctor-assisted suicides became public and prevalent. In the last few years, one state, Oregon, has passed a law permitting doctor-assisted suicides. The slide has begun.

CONTEMPORARY BATTLE LINES

Today, the hot topics of abortion, homosexuality, and euthanasia are not nearly so hot anymore. The public battle lines have moved from "Is homosexuality right or wrong?" to "Can businesses grant health coverage to same-sex partners of employees?" Depictions of homosexuals on television are very common and in most cases, very positive. Homosexuality is well on its way to being normalized.

The abortion rates have dropped slightly in the past couple of years, but the estimates are that 1.25 million unborn children are killed each year in the United States in order to protect women's rights. Certainly there are ethical questions about what to do when the life of the mother is genuinely at risk, but *life* is now defined as "quality of life," not "life and death," so the door is wide open to abort based on the mother's convenience. Challenges have been and continue to be raised against *Roe v. Wade,* but abortion remains entrenched in our national culture.

The value of human life is in the vise of a strange paradox in our society. On one hand, medicine has made such incredible advances that many diseases and injuries, which only a few years ago caused death, can now be healed. Organ transplants are commonplace. Bypass heart surgery saves hundreds of lives each day. Powerful antibiotics cure infections that used to kill. All this is in sharp contrast to the fact that until the early part of this century, fully half of all children died by their fifth birthday, and disease ravaged whole communities almost like the dreaded plagues. In the years shortly after World War I, for instance, a flu epidemic killed almost 22 million people, mostly in Europe and America. Today, antibiotics and hospital care prevent such outbreaks, and we are shocked when the flu kills a few dozen elderly people. Look at the gravestones of one hundred years ago, and see the sad reality of death in families. It was a common, almost expected, visitor. In contrast, modern medicine makes us feel that death should never touch us. We feel we should be beyond its clutches.

Now turn on the television. Go to a movie. People are blown to bits, knifed, machine-gunned, drowned, and obliterated in a zillion different ways—for our amusement. What does this dichotomy say to our young people, and to you and me? I believe it makes us think that death is only a fantasy, and medicine will protect us from it. This conception dulls our sense that each man and woman ultimately faces eternity. It robs us of the immediacy of purpose because we think medicine's miracles will always give us another chance. No, I'm not saying that modern medicine is evil. The new procedures and powerful drugs are wonderful gifts from God, and we need to see them as coming from His hand to enable us to serve Him more fully for a little longer. It's too easy to look to medicine instead of to God for eternity. I'm afraid the dual messages of the triumph of medicine and the cheapness of human life in the media have undercut our sense of the reality of God and of judgment.

Barna's survey contains sobering statistics about the perspectives of young people who attend our churches and youth groups every week. Here are some of his findings:

- Marriage and family—only 48 percent of these church youths say they want a marriage like that of their parents. Two-thirds believe divorce is the preferable option for parents who no longer love each other. The same percentage prefer a "no risk, no commitment" form of family instead of the traditional bonds.

- Sex—by graduation from high school, 27 percent of our youths have experienced sexual intercourse, 20 percent think sex between unmarried people is acceptable behavior, and 46 percent believe love, not marriage, makes sex acceptable.

- Ethics—85 percent of church youths believe in situational ethics: "What's right for you isn't necessarily what's right for me." Thirty-eight percent believe that their experience is more valuable than any objective standard of truth. Only 9 percent agreed with all seven "pro-truth" statements in the survey.

Barna's survey was extensive, but I want to highlight selected statements and responses from one part, "What Church Kids Believe":

- A person can experience a relationship with God personally.
  Agree 84 percent / Disagree 5 percent / Not sure 11 percent

- The Bible is totally accurate in all of its teaching.
  Agree 71 percent / Disagree 10 percent / Not sure 20 percent

- The Christian faith is relevant to the way I live today.
  Agree 70 percent / Disagree 12 percent / Not sure 19 percent

- The Christian churches in my area are relevant to the way I live today.
  Agree 56 percent / Disagree 19 percent / Not sure 25 percent

- No one can really prove which religion is absolutely true.
  Agree 40 percent / Disagree 34 percent / Not sure 25 percent

- The devil, or Satan, is not a living being, but is a symbol of evil.
  Agree 31 percent / Disagree 49 percent / Not sure 20 percent

- If a person is generally good, or does enough good things for others during their life, they will earn a place in Heaven.
  Agree 22 percent / Disagree 62 percent / Not sure 16 percent

- It does not matter what religious faith you follow because all faiths teach similar lessons.
  Agree 21 percent / Disagree 54 percent / Not sure 25 percent

- Jesus sometimes made mistakes.
  Agree 17 percent / Disagree 67 percent / Not sure 16 percent

- All good people, whether or not they consider Jesus Christ to be their Savior, will live in heaven after they die.
  Agree 13 percent / Disagree 69 percent / Not sure 18 percent

Perhaps the most significant readings in this list are that only about 50 percent of the churched young people in the survey believe their churches are relevant to their lives, and that only 70 percent believe their personal faith is relevant. That means almost one in three young people in our churches doesn't make the connection between faith and life. And these are the young people who have enough desire and commitment to come to youth group and church week after week!

The study shows that those who do not accept truth as the basis for life and decision making are 36 percent more likely to lie to a parent, 48 percent more likely to cheat on an exam, twice as likely to try to hurt someone physically, twice as likely to watch pornography, twice as likely to get drunk, more than twice as likely to steal, three times more likely to use illegal drugs, six times more likely to attempt suicide, 65 percent more likely to mistrust people, twice as likely to be disappointed, twice as likely to be angry, and twice as likely to lack purpose in life.[2]

STILL, THEY THIRST FOR TRUTH

Though the concept of truth has taken a beating in recent years, Millennials long for spiritual nourishment and meaning. God has made us all, Pascal said, with a "God-shaped vacuum" in our hearts. Nothing else can fill it. The existentialist movement of the late '60s vastly broadened our notion of who God is. The New Age movement of the '80s and '90s has brought that existentialist concept of God into the mainstream of American life. Walk into any major bookstore and you'll find a vast New Age section with hundreds of titles about how astrology, time travel, out-of-body experiences, séances, channeling, and dozens of other techniques can tap into modern spirituality. As propositional truth has come under attack, New Age "truths" have elbowed their way into popular books, movies, television programs, and every other part of our culture. Some are promoted by thinly veiled charlatans; others by the latest marketing techniques. They appear attractive, and they are garnering the following of millions. Our concept of God has broadened to our great detriment and shame.

A friend of mine told me that he visited India several years ago with a group from Campus Crusade for Christ. In New Delhi, the group met with a leading pastor from that city. The pastor told them wonderful stories of men and women whose lives had been changed by Christ. The group then talked about how to do evangelism in that predominantly Hindu culture. They discussed the use of a translation of *The Four Spiritual Laws* in Hindi, and they asked the New Delhi pastor for his input. He said, "Your booklet begins, 'God loves you and has a wonderful plan for your life.' In my culture, people don't know which 'god' you are talking about, so the booklet confuses them. I suggest you add another law at the beginning to define who our God is. Then they will understand the message more clearly." We have the same problem in the culture of the Millennials today.

Satan realizes that if he can destroy kids, he can destroy a whole culture, a whole generation. By eroding truth, he is creating a generation without a moral memory. It's not time for business as usual in our world. We need to recognize the slide of truth into the wastebasket of our culture and do what has to be done to change that trend. Coca-Cola spends tens of millions of dollars each year to convince teenagers that Coke is "the Real Thing." What kind of commitment are we making to make sure teenagers know Jesus is the *only* thing?

7

Isolation, Fragmentation, and Drift

Private optimism, public pessimism. I trust me; I just don't trust you. This perspective is common among Xers, and it dominates the hearts and minds of Millennials. One commentator stated,

> Americans feel good about pursuing their own personal lives (in families, neighborhoods, and jobs) according to their own lights during an era of relative prosperity. But Americans realize that along with limitless personal empowerment, the nation is experiencing a mood of civic decay and cultural exhaustion that cannot easily be reversed. People expect the moment will arrive when all the public claims we now defer and deny will take an urgent priority over the piecemeal fragmentation of the 1990s.[1]

GROWING CONCERN

A recent Gallup poll confirms this view. Only 10 percent of the people polled believe America is improving, and only 1 percent say that improvement is strong. In contrast, 50 percent of those responding see the country as declining, and more than 20 percent believe this decline is steep. A majority of people in our country are "worried" or "upset" about social trends: 60 percent are concerned about the American family, 59 percent about the ethical-moral condition of the nation, 56 percent about the economy, 54 percent about public education, and 50 percent about our national government. In fact, 70 percent believe the statement: "Most elected officials don't care what people like me think."

The study demonstrates the differences between the outlooks toward the presidency in each generation. In 1966, 41 percent of the Boomers and their parents had "a great deal of confidence" in the president. By 1976, after the Vietnam War and Watergate, only 23 percent held that high view. Today, only 13 percent have high regard for the presidency.[2] This recent figure is ironic because President Clinton's personal approval rating is the highest for any president ever, even though he has endured harsh skepticism over the morality of his personal life.

Craig Davis is a youth minister and John Haddad is a Young Life director. These men told me about the kids in their youth groups and at the local high school. John commented, "Kids at school are more cliquish than I've ever seen them. They've always gravitated into groups, but never like this."

Craig agreed, "Yeah, but there doesn't seem to be the suspicion and animosity between groups like in the past. Not many of them seem to care that they are excluded from a particular group." John nodded as Craig summed up the situation, "They are comfortable with these fragmented groups. That's the norm now."

FACTORS CONTRIBUTING TO ISOLATION

The widespread erosion of confidence in civic institutions combined with implied (or real) threats from media exposure to murders, rapes, and terrorism, the lack of a driving purpose, continued high divorce rates, abortion, and STDs, along with economic prosperity that provides comfort and options—all these blend together to create isolation, fragmentation, and drift among the Millennials.

Ironically the passionate tolerance of this generation has

contributed to their isolation. As the concept that "all perspectives are equally valid" has taken root, there are fewer ideological rallying points, fewer hopes and dreams in common, fewer things strangers can use to agree on and form a bond. If everything is valid, then young people (and older ones, too) become confused. They withdraw, retreating to the safety of aloneness or the haven of the relative few who agree with them and won't condemn them for what they believe.

As we have seen, the Millennials' preoccupation with computers also contributes to their isolation. Sure, some of them communicate often with people on chat lines, but 97 percent of communication is found not in the words alone, but in tone of voice, gestures, and the look on the other person's face—none of which is a part of chat rooms.

The image of this generation is of a big rock being pounded by a sledgehammer. Some blows seem to bounce off, but slowly, surely, repeated hits create cracks in the stone. Sooner or later, chunks break off. Repeated hammer blows shatter them into even smaller pieces. The blows of the sledgehammer are all the forces we've examined in this book. To be sure, they have crept up on us in the last few decades, and they don't seem at all like sharp hammer blows. But if we look at these forces in light of the long sweep of history, they have appeared suddenly with incredible force—just like the blows of a hammer.

The sense of isolation among Millennials isn't a desperate thing. Many of them actually feel pretty comfortable with it. It's all they've ever known. The erosion of trust during the Xers' childhood now is a part of the very air they breathe. The paradox is that their pessimism and skepticism exist in spite of many, many very positive efforts on the part of parents and government to provide and protect. The introduction of the V-chip is designed to let parents screen out violent, sexual, or any other objectionable television programs. These early years of the Internet have seen an incredible increase in the accessibility of pornography, but parents, government, and a myriad of organizations are committed to making the Internet safe for children. Government on all levels has been, and will continue to be, riveted on meeting the needs of children. A movement is under way among judges not to allow divorce so quickly and easily, and "deadbeat dads" are being tracked down and prosecuted by zealous state attorney generals to make them pay child support.

Strauss and Howe see other trends:

> Children will not attach themselves so exclusively to mothers, many of whom will be working. Instead, they will attach themselves to a rotating array of substitute parents (often male) who represent the community. Like the offspring of a well-run kibbutzim, Millennials will grow up to be sociable and team-oriented adolescents but will strike adults as somewhat bland, conformist, and dependent on others to reach judgments.[3]

EXTREME FADS

But not all Millennials are bland. One of the rages among adolescents today is body piercing. Walk in the mall for a few minutes (it won't take long, I assure you), and you'll see kids with every part of their bodies pierced and tattooed. Ears? That's old-fashioned, but some put a dozen rings in all parts of their ears. More trendy piercings include eyelids, noses, tongues, and belly buttons, but genital piercings are now popular too. And tattoos aren't just for Harley riders anymore. Lots of girls are getting their ankles or shoulders tattooed, and of course, guys get their arms done up in style. For the majority of Millennials who pierce their noses or get a tattoo, it's not much different from pegged pants and ducktails in the '60s. It's just the thing to do right now to be different.

But a more alarming aspect of all this trend is self-mutilation. Psychologist Lynn Ponton, author of *The Romance of Risk: Why Teenagers Do the Things They Do,* believes kids today are bored, so they burn, cut, and disfigure themselves to get high. Ponton states, "There is less for [young people] to do today in risk-taking, so they're turning to their own bodies." For some, the goal is an outlandish new body form, such as knobby growths on the head that become horns, or taking out ribs so the waist can be fifteen or sixteen inches. But for others, the pain involved is the goal itself. An article in the *San Francisco Chronicle* described one girl, Amy, who has scarred hands from digging her fingernails into them for years. She also broke windows in her mother's house in order to cut herself. "I like pain," she says flatly. "Pain is like a drug. It can be either a good or a bad drug. It can either enhance or destroy."

The cult of pain in San Francisco welcomed Amy and her friend Ivy who remembered, "When I found there was an actual scene here, it made me feel that I was OK. I wasn't a freak." The group asked her to be branded on stage at a club, and she agreed. "It was going to another level. How much can I take? It's like being in another state of mind." Ivy was branded on her upper arm in four sections, searing her skin each time for a few seconds. "I liked it. I liked the smell. That was part of it." When the brand marks began to fade several months later, Ivy had them done again.

Like Amy and Ivy, an estimated two million adolescents in the United States are self-mutilators. The writer for the *Chronicle* stated,

> Psychologists say that cutting and other self-injury provide temporary relief from intense feelings of anxiety, anger or depression—a theory that seems supported by science. Cutting the skin releases beta-endorphins, the body's natural pain-killer. The endorphins can actually boost one's mood. Indeed, many who return repeatedly to the piercing shops describe an elation during and after the pain. Over time, a person usually must inflict more frequent and more acute pain in order to achieve the same sensation.

Dr. Armando Favazza, professor of psychiatry at the University of Missouri-Columbia Medical School, calls this practice "a morbid form of self-help."[4]

DESPERATE FOR LOVE

I see thousands of teenagers who desperately want to be loved, who feel so lonely that they can't stand it any longer. I received this letter after one of our conferences:

Dear Dawson,

I need to be loved. I've prayed to God that I could have assurance. And I still feel alone. Family is important? How so when you become the shadow in your own house. Relationships are to fulfill the other part of you. I am supposed to have a significant other. I'm sorry but I have been ready to die for love for the past few weeks. A hug could do wonders, but 5 minutes later I feel lonely. No one has said, "Sandra, I love you" and meant it fully in the past 2 or 3 weeks. I want help, yes. But I am stuck in my ways. I despise change. I need you to tell me how to make my mother and sister love me again.

You're my last hope,

Sandra

And others communicate their sense of abandonment in other ways. I received this beautiful and haunting poem from a lonely young person:

No one sees
Me fall to my knees
I drop to the floor

I cannot run anymore
I've run for so long
So many things have gone wrong
I don't know how, I don't know why
All I know is I want to die
Oh God! What should I do
I want to begin a life anew
Without any enemies, problems, or depression
My problems have become my obsession
No one hears
My bittersweet tears
No one cares
No one dares
No one knows
I guess that's the way it goes
Every day
I try a new way
To lose my sadness
But this world is madness
I haven't a clue
Of what I should do.

One night on our radio program, I received a call from a girl who was obviously distressed and lonely. Susan told me, "Well, my parents, they've been like going through this divorce for a long time. They got separated like two years ago and then they got back together, but . . . my dad, he . . . like . . . would like beat me and stuff."

I asked, "A lot?"

"Yeah. My mom used to work nights, or at the second shift so she would be gone from when I got home from school until I would . . . after I would go to bed, and my dad, he'd come home and he'd like freak out and take out all of his anger on me and my sister every night almost."

"So you were getting beaten almost every night?"

"Yeah," she said softly.

"How old were you at the time?"

"Well, it, um, almost all my life up until two years ago, until I was twelve."

Susan had bottled up her hurt and anger. As we continued to talk, she told me, "I'm afraid if I start really crying, it will just all gush everywhere . . . I'm terrified for that to happen. I might never stop."

We continued to talk, and I let her share her deep hurts with me and the radio audience. I told her about experiencing God's forgiveness, so she could forgive her father for hurting her. She also needed to forgive her mother for not protecting her from her dad. I assured her that those who were listening would be praying for her, and I directed her to call our Help Line to get additional help. Millions of young people feel disconnected from—or worse, battered by—family and friends. They believe they have nowhere to turn.

FILLING UP THE HOLE WITH THINGS

Studies show that many teenagers are more materialistic than in years past. The affluence of the economy and the lack of external purposes leave them with plenty of money but no one to spend it on, except themselves. They tend to be individualistic and gravitate toward new brands as they spend almost $70 billion a year on clothes, jewelry, CDs, entertainment, and cars.[5]

Some teenagers are heavily involved in extreme sports such as BASE jumping (in which daredevils parachute from fixed objects typically three hundred to two thousand feet high), and even those who aren't involved think it's cool. Snowboarding is probably the hottest sport among teenagers today, and it is becoming immensely popular at virtually every ski resort in the country.

A strong trend among Millennials is to work during the school year—a trend that worries educators and political scientists who assert that teenagers who work have less time for studies, relationships, and involvement in clubs and sports. Teenagers, however, insist that they work so they can have enough money to be independent of their parents. Some educators have a different perspective. Ron Young, who has been teaching government and social studies at Stebbins High School in Riverside, California, for thirty-two years, stated, "They are supporting a much higher material level than previous generations. It's not just the car now, they have to have the stereo, the phone, the computer, the right clothes. I think this is one of the reasons they are not as interested and involved in politics and their community."[6]

Help Me Understand

So, let's see. Millennials are pampered more by their parents and by government than in many years, but they don't trust them. They are in the most affluent country the world has ever known, but they are bored. They have incredible technology at their fingertips at home and at school, but they have poor relationships and feel alone. Government institutions aren't trusted, but Millennials lack any sense of purpose. Isolation, fragmentation, and drift.

"We don't have anything to fight for," a sixteen-year-old lamented. "The World War II generation had a war, and the Baby Boomers had Vietnam."

"Yeah," a friend interrupted, "what we need is a good war."

Or maybe a Savior.

8

4-N Language

Teenagers have always developed their own language. Some of us remember terms we used way back when: *copacetic, groovy, hip,* and *square. Cool* has been around forever. For some reason, it seems to transcend all cultural barriers. And if you're really old, you can remember when kids said "L-seven" if they wanted to tell their friends somebody was square. Today's teenagers have their own words for good and bad, but the issue of communication is much deeper than a couple of words or catchphrases. Different values pervade their communication.

Have you traveled abroad and had difficulties communicating a really important piece of information or a question, such as, "Where's the bathroom?" If you travel to Western Europe, the language may be a problem, but if you can find the right words, communication is pretty simple. But travel to countries where the values and customs are genuinely different from our own, and simple communication is much more complicated. Go to an Arab country, but don't look at a woman in the eyes. Eye contact between unmarried people is considered almost adulterous in some cultures. Go to Thailand, but don't cross your legs and let the bottoms of your feet be seen. Showing the soles of your feet is terribly offensive to them. And when you go to some cultures and have a meal with new friends, it is considered very rude not to let out a big belch to show how much you liked dinner! (I know some high school boys who would be considered very gracious there!)

DÉJÀ VU

Some historians compare today's young people with those of the 1920s. In many ways, the situations are similar, and the response of kids in both eras is strikingly consistent. One authority wrote that the 1920s "was an era of rapid technological change, egocentric celebrities, widening class divisions . . . and weak political leadership. A fun-filled financial boom was framed in pessimistic debates over drugs, sex, money, cynicism, violence, immigration, and the family."[1] Sounds familiar, doesn't it? We are seeing the same issues on the front page of today's newspapers, in today's schools, and in today's marketplace.

COMPUTER-SPEAK

You and I want to communicate with today's young people. I know you do because you bought this book and you're reading it! To talk effectively, we need to understand their customs and culture, almost as though communicating with them is speaking a foreign language. Kids today are plugged in. Computers and other electronics are their way of life, not add-on luxuries. They are used to discussing the latest software and power capabilities of new computers just as, well, some of us used to talk about a Mustang's carburetor. Schools recognize the need to equip students to be able to compete in the modern job market, so they are providing (and in most cases, requiring) computer classes for high school students. If we want to communicate with them, we need to stay abreast of the latest technology.

Some of us are reactionaries. We like the way things used to be, when we had adding machines instead of Pentium IIs, LPs instead of CDs, and *To Kill a Mockingbird* instead of *Pulp Fiction*. Yes, things were simpler then. And it's hard to stay up with the latest technology. But if we want to communicate, we need to at least give it a try. One way is to let them teach us. We can swallow our pride, pull up a chair, and ask a few questions about how the systems work, which program is best, and which game has the most pizzazz. It will take some time to learn, but it may provide an open door to communication with a teenager.

THE CULT OF TOLERANCE

Another key word in today's teenagers' vocabulary is *tolerance*. I said they are passionately tolerant, that is, totally intolerant of anybody who takes sides or says something is right or wrong. For those of us who are Boomers, and even for some who are Xers, the lack of absolutes is baffling. It's easy to lose patience with kids who are adamant only about the absence of anything to be adamant about.

Recently I heard someone say, "People today are more concerned about being judgmental about sin than they are about the sin itself." Today's kids consider being judgmental one of the worst possible character traits. The public discourse about President Clinton's alleged sexual escapades clearly shows this perspective. Many, many Americans say they don't trust the president, but his behavior "isn't anybody's business but his own," and we "shouldn't judge him because we've all lied at one time or another." Even in the midst of fresh disclosures from Kathleen Willey about the president groping her, Clinton's popularity rating continued at an all-time high.

Passionate about tolerance. That's our culture. If we want to communicate with these people, we have to go beyond stating only our black-and-white opinions. We must be willing to fight through our disgust at others' lack of clarity to find common ground. Perhaps talking about consequences is a beginning point in many discussions. In most cases, the positive or negative consequences of behavior seem fairly clear. Maybe we can open a dialogue at that point and go beyond cause and effect to discuss underlying principles.

Not long ago in talking with teenagers about morality, I brought up Bill Clinton and Monica Lewinsky. Clinton, I pointed out, said that he hadn't had sex with her because he narrowly defines sex as intercourse. Bill Clinton proves the modern way of thinking: the truth is whatever you want it to be. While I explained this perspective, there was a hushed silence in the crowd that I would mention oral sex. After a few minutes, they began to laugh. They didn't laugh because I was speaking about sex. They were laughing at President Clinton. As a Christian speaker, I often disagree with what Bill Clinton says and does, but I'm very careful now when I talk to teenagers about this simply because they laugh at him and thereby laugh at the presidency.

Today's young people are very spiritual, but they lack focus. New Age, Mormonism, Jehovah's Witness, Buddhism, Hinduism, Native American, and literally any other spiritual paradigm are attractive to people who don't have a sense of historical or propositional truth. Years ago I heard a pastor talk about evangelism. He said we need to find common ground when we talk to people about Christ. If they are interested in humanistic philosophy, we need to understand the philosophy and find points where we agree. From that point, no matter how meager the beginning, we can build rapport. For many of us, teenagers' glad acceptance of any and all spiritual perspectives is abhorrent. We react and tell them they're wrong! And they often are. But we don't win too many through condemnation. Jesus was harsh with stiff, legalistic religious leaders, but He was patient and kind (and still truthful) with people who sought spiritual enlightenment.

Today's young people have a natural negative reaction toward parents, teachers, government, and any other authority. That has always been the case as teenagers become individuals and adults, but today, the lack of trust is deeper and wider than in most other generations. Students today have lots of doubts, and too often, adults are answering questions the kids aren't even asking. Students are asking *why* and *what*. Many adults don't realize the kids are struggling at that level, and they are answering *how* questions. Many young people feel very comfortable giving their opinions about all kinds of issues. A friend of mine says they aren't afraid of being wrong because they don't really value what's right and wrong. And Millennials are as interested in the political process today as they are in looking at our high school annual pictures! Both seem equally irrelevant to them. They don't trust authority, including government. They don't see how politics can make any difference at all, so it's not worth even trying to become involved.

THREE CHOICES

We have three choices in how we respond to Millennials:

1. *Condemnation.* A friend of mine from the West Coast was speaking and singing at a church in Alabama. He was giving them both barrels, but the kids just weren't catching his drift. They barely sang the songs. They barely laughed at his jokes. They barely responded to anything he said. Finally my friend stopped his music and sneered at the big room full of kids, "I travel all over the country, and I've never gotten this response on a song. What's wrong? Are you too tired to believe this?" They knew exactly what he was saying. What he really meant was, "Are you just a bunch of losers?"

I had a little talk with my friend and explained that the Alabama young people weren't used to his West Coast ways. He needed to win them with warmth, not condemn them for not responding the way he wanted them to respond. To his credit, he changed his tune and loved those kids until they warmed up to him. He had a big hurdle to overcome, one that he had created by his condemning tone and harsh words.

In the stereotypical adult-adolescent conflict, adults are often mystified by the behavior and attitudes of teenagers. Next they become discouraged, and then angry. Dialogue breaks down early in the process, and each retreats to an armed camp to hurl angry epithets at the other. Not a pretty sight. Common, but not pretty.

It may not seem possible, but teenagers today may be even more sensitive to criticism than teens of past generations because of the culture's emphasis on tolerance. Criticism, absolutes, and resulting condemnation are taboo in this age. When adults are perceived as judgmental, kids react. This reaction, of course, only fuels the adults' anger at the adolescents' unwillingness to listen, so anger and condemnation escalate on both sides.

Jesus stepped out of heaven into a foreign land. He saw all the filth and the self-righteousness that destroy lives and dishonor the Father. He could have blasted every man, woman, and child on earth in His righteous wrath, but He didn't. He said, "I did not come to judge the world but to save the world" (John 12:47). Sure, He spoke the truth to a people who sometimes accepted that truth but often did not. He never wavered in His message, but He made sure to build bridges of understanding and kindness with anyone who would respond to His invitation. Sometimes I think of the people who felt comfortable with Jesus: hated tax gatherers, despised prostitutes, outcasts, adulteresses, people condemned by the "socially acceptable" crowd. But they didn't feel condemned by the Holy One, God in the flesh, the Alpha and the Omega who was, is, and will always be perfect righteousness. Even those who were farthest away from His perfect law felt drawn to Him, His message, His truth, and His salvation.

It is much easier to just condemn those who don't hold to truth and right living, just as the Pharisees and Sadducees condemned those who gravitated to Jesus. I'm sure the religious leaders felt good about upholding truth in their scathing denunciation of sinners, but they lost their audience.

But condemnation is not the only easy way to respond.

2. *Accommodation.* Another easy (but opposite) response is to change our own values and become like the culture too. Some do this in the name of love, because they feel that affirming young people's beliefs, becoming like them, and not making waves are loving things to do. Those who hold this view may quote Paul's statement, "To the Jews I became as a Jew, that I might win Jews; to those who are under the law, as under the law, that I might win those who are under the law" (1 Cor. 9:20). In practice, we can accommodate both truth and behavior. We adopt some of the broad spirituality of the New Age and Hinduism (or any of the other myriad versions of spirituality out there today), and we try to see the good in these religious experiences. Or we may try to act like young people, wear their styles, and talk their lingo to relate more effectively.

I've seen some really old people (about my age) who think the best way to relate to students is to become like them. They dress like them, talk like them, listen to their music, affirm their perspectives, and generally try to be retroteenagers. Maybe a couple of people can pull that off, but most of the ones I've seen don't get very far with Millennials. The students see right through the charade—no matter how well-intentioned it may be—and they back away. It just doesn't work to try to be somebody you aren't. The vast majority of young people value adults who are honest and who have integrity, not those who change their lives to fit in. They see enough of that at school.

Accommodation is attractive because it takes the Millennial culture seriously and makes a valiant attempt to communicate love to young people. However, it sacrifices the distinctives of truth in order to relate. Young people today need to feel understood, but they also need the life-changing presence, truth, and power of God to be unleashed in their lives. And they don't need a bunch of old people trying to look and act as they do. They can spot a phony in a heartbeat!

There is a better way.

3. *Empathy.* The apostle John told us that Jesus came to us as the embodiment of "grace and truth." Both. Not one or the other. He didn't use truth to harshly condemn, and He didn't let His infinite love turn His truth into mush to make it more palatable. Two passages of Scripture tell us a lot about how Jesus was able to relate lovingly and honestly with people. The writer to the Hebrews told us that Jesus "walked a mile in our shoes": "For we do not have a High Priest [Jesus] who cannot sympathize with our weaknesses, but was in all points tempted as we are, yet without sin" (Heb. 4:15). Jesus faced every fear, temptation, and hope that we do. He understands because He walked the same path we walk. So then, let us "come boldly to the throne of grace, so that we may obtain mercy and find grace to help in time of need" (Heb. 4:16).

In his letter to the believers at Philippi, Paul implored readers to have the same attitude as that of Christ Jesus, who existed in perfect glory and power, but "made Himself of no reputation, taking the form of a bondservant . . . humbled Himself and became obedient to the point of death" (Phil. 2:5–11). He didn't remain smug and safe. He took the risk—a risk that cost Him His life—to communicate grace and truth.

Jesus is our example of how to communicate with Millennials (and anybody else, for that matter). Just as Jesus spent countless hours with people to listen, watch, and interact, we need to listen and watch far more, and speak far less. Quick to listen; slow to speak—that's a good, biblical principle for every relationship. Listening and asking questions don't mean we agree with what we hear. We may not agree with much of what is said, but our faces will tell them whether we condemn them or not. As we understand more, compassion will replace condemnation in our hearts. We won't react as much. Instead, we will have just as much zeal for truth, but we will have plowed the fields so that the seeds will fall on more fertile soil. Condemnation makes people like concrete. Compassion, gentleness, and kindness can—over time perhaps—make people receptive to truth.

Several years ago, students started writing me notes and walking up to the stage unannounced to give them to me. We receive several hundred notes per conference. Why would they do that? They're desperate. Ninety-five percent of the notes are poignant descriptions of their pain. At one particular event, hundreds of teenagers came down the aisles of the church to make a commitment to Christ. I watched the Lord working in the dear young people's lives, and I saw that one girl was trying to get up to the front to speak to me. Her expression showed that she was desperate. She was yelling to me, but I couldn't hear her over the music. Finally she pushed her way to the stage, and I heard her yell, "Did you get my message?"

Suddenly I remembered and yelled back, "Yes, I got it!"

Her countenance changed instantly. Knowing I had gotten her message and understood her meant the world to her. It means the world to each of us to know someone has listened and understood.

Unfortunately I don't always listen. At the end of a summer camp years ago, I was ready to go home. It was hot, I had spoken a bazillion times, and I was exhausted. A young girl came to me and told me she had been sexually abused by a man in her neighborhood. I didn't want to hear all that. I wanted to get a Coke and take a break! So I didn't listen. I told her to "just get over it" and "move on with your life." My tired clichés only hurt the poor girl even more. Her anger grew, and she stalked out of the room.

Those two encounters are deeply written on my memory. They tell me that listening is perhaps the most important thing we can do for someone—even for a professional speaker! The best way to love people is to hear what they have to say, to assure them we care and we understand.

When we listen, we will find that Millennials have different thought processes from those of older generations. They are used to rapid processors and instant decisions. *Wait* isn't in their vocabulary! They have access to far more information than we ever did, and they are used to storing it on disks (floppy, Zip, and now Jazz) for future use. They don't feel they need to remember many things since they can access whatever they need at any time.

As we have seen, their values are different. As the postmodern and post-Christian trends continue to take over, sin will become less and less clearly defined. Even today, people wonder, "Whatever happened to sin?" And, we might add, righteousness. Take time to listen deeply to what they believe. Don't correct too quickly or you will probably lose them.

BE STRAIGHT, BE REAL

By all means, be straight with them. When I speak to young people, I often say, "Look, I know you don't trust me. I know you've been hurt, and I know you're angry. I know you've been told not to trust authority, and I know that I'm old. You can see that! But God's message is not old, and His answers are fresh and alive. You will see that I love you—that's why I'm going to tell you the truth." When we speak to Millennials, we need to let them know that we know how they feel, and we care about them. We understand why they feel that way, and nothing is going to stop us from loving them. And if we really care about them, we'll tell them the straight, unvarnished truth—about God, about themselves, and about the consequences of their choices. They really appreciate our candor when it is combined with genuine love for them.

And share your own experiences. Millennials value actual experience more than propositional truth. What you feel and what you did are often more important to them than the principles you acted upon. Don't see that as a threat. See it as an open door to relate, to identify with them.

A friend of mine went to a national youth conference of a very liberal denomination. The vast majority of the young people there were deeply spiritual, but not Christians. One girl shared in her small groups about how meaningful a blue ball had been to her, how it had brought her closer to Mother God. Others followed a syncretism of Muhammad, Jesus, and Buddha. Some were into astrology. My friend began sharing truth from the Scriptures, and she was met with instant, violent defensiveness. She knew she was right, but she decided to change her approach. She began sharing how Christ had changed her life, how real He is to her, and how He is her best friend who is with her always. Suddenly the other kids' eyes lit up. Their whole countenances changed. They desperately wanted what my friend has! And they followed her around for the rest of the conference asking a zillion questions about how to have that kind of relationship with Christ. She shared the same truth with them then, but they were much more willing to receive it.

At first, she was perceived as condemning, and they shut her out. When she shared her experiences and listened to them without accommodating and changing what she believed, she won their respect and, ultimately, their hearts. We would do well to follow her example in communicating to a foreign culture.

9

Real Spirituality

The youth culture is changing. Our assumptions about young people need to change too. Dean Borgman, who holds the Culpepper Chair of Youth Ministry at Gordon-Conwell Theological Seminary, observes we are in "the second great watershed" of youth culture. The first watershed, Borgman states, occurred following World War II when the entire concept of a "teen culture" took root. Before that time, children who became old enough to work assumed adult responsibilities overnight, but in the flush of prosperity after the war, adolescents no longer needed to work. They had time, money, and energy. They developed their own styles and subculture. Teenagers had arrived! Youth ministry became a targeted emphasis of churches, and they picked up the enthusiasm. They attracted kids and entertained them by having music, skits, short talks, and lots of fun. That model has been in place for the past half century.

A new wave in youth culture, and a new model of ministry is gradually replacing the rally model. Borgman notes, "Their Walkmans, VCRs, and cable TV have given these kids an artificial and superficial home in the absence of parents."[1] Family life and learning styles are not the only things that change our assumptions. The postmodern and post-Christian influences have eroded the assumptions we can make about the spirituality of today's young people. In decades past, we could assume that if we taught the Scriptures, listeners could fairly easily assimilate that truth. They had "hands" to grab it and "mental shelves" to put it on. That's no longer true for many, many students. Their lack of respect for authority and the absence of absolutes make them wonder, "Why should I follow what these people are saying? I might find something I like better tomorrow."

EXPERIENCE OR TRUTH?

Young people value experience more than propositional truth. That doesn't mean we throw away truth (see the next chapter), but we have to come through the door they have opened to us. That door is experience. Think back on times when you felt particularly close to the Lord, times when God miraculously met your need, times when something couldn't be explained apart from the supernatural movement of God's hand. (If you've read this far in the book, I have no doubt that you've had those kinds of experiences. Other folks have put the book down by now!) How did these times affect you? I can think of several instances. In each one, my faith was strengthened, and I was drawn closer to the Father. That's what I'm talking about, not some truth-void, New Age, flaky experience of people contemplating mushrooms to feel closer to God! Our genuine experience of God's presence affirms the validity of the Word of God and galvanizes our faith.

Experience of course must always be inextricably linked with truth. We live in a day in which hundreds of "religions" are available to anybody and everybody. Go to your local bookstore and walk down the religion and the New Age aisles. You'll see an incredible number of books that espouse the benefits of every major world religion, spin-offs of those, astrology, necromancy (talking to the dead), prophecy of end times based on scores of "prophets," cults such as Scientology and EST, and one of the hottest new lines of religion, Native American spirituality. All of them promise "spiritual experience," so what we offer may not seem as novel and unique as you may think.

INTERVIEWS AND ENCOUNTERS

At our speaking events, we have been doing something that has proved to be powerful with the kids. We take a microphone out to the audience to let the young people speak. We also have image magnification screens. The camera puts their pictures on the big screens, so it doesn't matter whether we have five hundred or five thousand—everybody can see the person speaking. I interview these kids about whatever issue I want to talk about. It is amazing how time and time again they just share their guts in front of the world. Their sharing gives me rich illustrations for the rest of the weekend because I key off what these students say. The students are absolutely quiet when their peers are talking because they realize the discussion is completely unrehearsed and real. These young people become the stars. The more you make a student a star, the more powerful the experience is going to be.

We have also had youth workers stand at the front of the stage facing the audience. We ask kids to bring things to these people that are keeping them from God—cigarettes, condoms, jewelry that may represent something that is against God, and anything else they may have with them that is an impediment to their walks with God. If they don't have it with them, they can write it out on a piece of paper or draw a picture of it (such as wrong friends or wrong boyfriend or girlfriend) and give it to a youth worker standing at the front. The kids respond by the hundreds. I often take some of these symbols and point them out to the crowd. This, too, is a gripping experience.

At one of our events in Birmingham, Alabama, hundreds of students brought down symbols of things that drove a wedge between them and God. One young man handed his KKK membership card to a youth worker at the front, who then handed it to me. The card described the right of white people to shoot blacks. It was a hunting license that used the *n* word over and over again. I read this card to the students, and you could have heard a pin drop. It was really intense.

The next morning, I asked the black students to come forward and face the audience. Then I asked the student who gave the KKK membership card to come forward and ask the black students for forgiveness. It was pretty risky, but I knew he wanted to do something like that or he wouldn't have come forward the day before. For a minute, no one in the huge auditorium moved a muscle. Finally in the balcony a young man stood up and made his way downstairs and then down the center aisle. He started at one end of the line of black people and asked each one for forgiveness for hating their race. I could see a genuine earnestness on his face.

When he finished, I asked if others wanted to come down front and confess their sin of racism too. About twenty-five students got up and came forward. All this took about forty minutes, but it was the most meaningful time of the entire conference. If you talk to those hundreds of students today, almost every one of them has forgotten what I talked about, but not a one of them has forgotten those forty minutes when fellow students confessed their sin of racism to those they have hated. I had been speaking about the Cross and forgiveness. The experience helped the young people understand and apply the truths in a deep and profound way. It got out of their notebooks and into their hearts.

In the last several years, I've seen something I've never seen before: kids walking down an aisle, coming to the altar to confess their sins in the middle of one of my talks. They come unannounced and unbidden. And now I stop in the middle of a talk and offer kids a chance to come to the altar to pray or to deal with whatever I just talked about. They feel they will experience more if they are closer to the stage.

SPIRITUAL FORMATION

When young people walk into our churches and youth groups today, what do they see? What do they feel? They seek God. They want the real thing, not just dry words and dead services. A movement seems to be welling up across the nation that speaks to this need for a genuine experience with Jesus. It is a movement based on a spiritual formation model. In his excellent book *Working the Angles: The Shape of Pastoral Integrity,* Eugene Peterson says that spiritual direction is the ministry that promotes this formation. It centers on finding God in every aspect of life, no matter how mundane. He writes, "Spiritual direction takes place when two people agree to give their full attention to what God is doing in one (or both) of their lives and seek to respond in faith." Peterson states there are

> three convictions [which] underpin these meetings: (1) God is always doing something: an active grace is shaping this life into a mature salvation; (2) responding to God is not sheer guesswork: the Christian community has acquired wisdom through the centuries that provides guidance; (3) each soul is unique: no wisdom can simply be applied without discerning the particulars of this life, this situation.[2]

The differences between this model and traditional youth ministry are shown in this chart:

TRADITIONAL MODEL	SPIRITUAL FORMATION MODEL
Knowledge	Intimacy with God
Communicate content	Facilitate experience
Entertain and teach	Equip people to notice, name, and nurture God's hand at work
Youth minister as hub	Team of mentors

The purpose of the youth ministry model of the past half

century was to communicate knowledge about God with the assumption that young people could grab that knowledge and make it their own. That assumption was valid in the lives of millions of young people up until a decade ago. The focus of the spiritual formation model is intimacy. It doesn't bypass knowledge, but always seeks to make that knowledge real in actual experience. The goal is a rich, real intimacy with God without making assumptions that kids can jump from knowledge to experience on their own. The question is, What changes lives? In years past, the knowledge we communicated changed lives because young people had enough spiritual handles to assimilate it and apply it. That is no longer true today.

The style of youth ministry was fun and games with a short talk at the end. Youth ministers became incredibly creative at inventing skits, contests, and other wacky things to draw kids to meetings, make them laugh, and then communicate a gem of truth. And it worked! Many of us reading these pages are thinking, *So what's wrong with that? That's how I became a Christian. That's how I grew in my faith. That's how I met my wife. Hey, it's a winner!* I'm not saying that style of ministry is wrong. It just isn't culturally relevant (or as relevant as it used to be). When television was in its infancy, and there were no cable television, VCRs, video games, or virtual reality, then swallowing goldfish was pretty cool! But today, youth ministries have an incredibly difficult time competing with the images kids see in all the media they watch every day. These images are sharp and quick. The new technology is unbelievable. And think what it will be like tomorrow! But technology can't provide people with one thing they desperately want: an experience with the God of grace. We can.

NOTICE, NAME, AND NURTURE

In the spiritual formation model, we help people pay attention to what God is already doing around them. Churches of every denomination and stripe are using *Experiencing God* by Henry

Blackaby and Claude King. This material identifies seven principles of spiritual life. The first one is: "God is always at work around you."[3] This is a simple—and revolutionary—concept. God is at work. If we look carefully enough, we will be able to see His hand move in our lives and circumstances. Hundreds of thousands of adults, and many young people, too, have learned to look for God's hand and, by extension, His heart. We *notice* what God is doing, we *name* it and identify it as the work of His hand, and we *nurture* both our experience of God and His continued work. Let's look at these.

An individual can ask himself, "How have I seen God at work today (or this week)?" or a youth leader can ask a group of students, "How have you seen God at work since we were together last (or at our retreat or in our outreach or another event)?" The assumption is clear and strong: God *is* at work. It is our privilege to stop and look to see what He is up to. That is noticing. Students then verbalize what they've seen God do. That's naming. They may observe, "I noticed that Jim asked a question about how he could know Christ," or "God worked in Sarah's parents' lives; they aren't going to divorce now," or "When we read Luke 15 tonight, I felt like I was the prodigal son returning home. I could feel the Father's forgiveness and love!" There certainly isn't a formula of how God is working in people's lives. At the same event at the same moment, God may be doing a myriad of things in different people's lives. At the moment someone voices how he has seen God at work, the leader can reinforce that perception, nurture the person's grasp of God's hand, and solidify the experience. He can draw the person out ("Tell us more"), link the observation to something someone else said ("You know, that's like what Frank saw God doing"), or simply affirm the person ("That's great! Good observation; I didn't see that").

The process of helping students notice, name, and nurture the work of God involves them directly in their own spiritual development. The youth pastor or volunteer is no longer filling up an empty pot. Instead, the leader becomes a fellow traveler who facilitates everyone's personal experience of God. Everyone becomes a participant, and everyone contributes to the others' experiences of God. It is a moving and powerful time. Of course, I'm not advocating that our youth ministries become monasteries and that all of us take vows of emotional poverty. We can still have plenty of fun, but at some point, we need to get quiet and reflect on how we see God at work.

ONE-MAN SHOW VS. A TEAM

In the traditional model, the youth minister has to be an expert in everything: funny man, outstanding speaker, counselor, fund-raiser, confidant, bus driver, astronaut . . . (Okay, I guess he doesn't have to do that, but close!) The pressure is enormous to please kids, parents, and other church staff by pulling off incredible events week after week while spending plenty of time with the family, paying bills on time, having a rich devotional life, and keeping the oil changed in the car. Is it any wonder that the average youth minister bails after eighteen months in the ministry? Some hardy and creative souls do this style of ministry very well, but even then, being the hub of the universe is a tough job.

The spiritual formation model relies on a team of mentors; each mentor is deeply involved in the lives of a few young people. Each one facilitates the formation of the spiritual life within the hearts of these young people. Some of these mentors may also dream up skits and supervise games, but their primary responsibility, their focused role, is the development of spiritual acuity within a few precious young lives.

This new approach to ministry is wonderfully affirming to the youth pastor's and volunteers' spiritual lives. They need to notice, name, and nurture the presence of Christ in their own lives so that their experiences will overflow in their ministries to students.

HELP THEM APPLY SCRIPTURE

Spiritual formation usually includes specific modes of prayer and Bible study. The varieties of forms for these are exceedingly broad. Some may choose the disciplines of the desert fathers or modern mystics such as Thomas Kelly, author of *A Testament of Devotion*. Most will use songs and choruses to get in step with the Spirit. And many will employ active Bible studies to help people experience the truth of Scripture more deeply. For instance, a youth group spent several weeks studying Luke 8:40–48, the story of Jesus healing the woman who had been bleeding for twelve years.

The first week, the youth pastor read the passage slowly twice while the students closed their eyes and imagined the scene. Then he asked them, "What stands out in the passage to you?" It was amazing that different people latched on to such different aspects of the story.

The next week, the youth pastor asked the students to pick one person in the story and put themselves in that person's place, then he read the story again twice. He asked them how they felt as the person they'd selected entered and participated in the scene. Once again, the responses were varied and profound. One said, "I identified with Peter. I felt impatient with Jesus for stopping for that woman when we were on our way to a synagogue official's house. If He healed the official's kid, He'd get a lot more press!" Another student picked up on that: "Yeah, I was Jairus, and I was really hacked off that Jesus stopped. My daughter was dying!" And another said, "I was the woman. I was desperate for help, so I reached out and touched the hem of His robe. But suddenly I was terrified by the attention. When Jesus said, 'Daughter,' I imagined Him saying it so tenderly and lovingly, my heart melted." The group basked in their shared insights, then the youth pastor asked them, "So how does this apply in your own experience, your own hurts, your own need for Jesus to come through for you?" That led to a rich conversation about their lives and how Jesus was meeting, or would meet, them as He met the woman or how He made them wait as He made Jairus wait or how He ignored the misunderstanding as Jesus ignored Peter while giving attention to the needy, bold, yet frightened woman.

The third week, the kids came in as usual, but when time for Bible study came around, they noticed a robe was draped over a chair in the room. They settled down as the youth pastor read the passage again. Then, quiet. In a few moments, the youth pastor walked over to the robe, knelt, and reached out to touch the hem. He stopped for a moment, then went back to his seat. A volunteer went to the robe a few moments later. Then another. Soon students were getting up and going to touch the hem of the robe. They remained in silent prayer for a while, then they shared what they were thinking and feeling. At the end, the youth pastor gave each person a piece of fabric to symbolize touching the hem, and he told each person, "Your faith has made you well. Go in peace."

These Bible study exercises focus on experience, not just knowledge. And similar activities can be developed to communicate virtually every truth and principle. These exercises allow the participants to do the typical observation, interpretation, and application, but in a creative, experiential context.

This kind of exercise works very well in high school and college groups because they see Christ as an integral part of their peer group. The concept of having a relationship with this incredible Friend is rich and real to them, and such exercises encourage them to experience Jesus Himself, not just truth about Jesus.

The spiritual formation model also gives appropriate attention to the ministry of the Holy Spirit to teach, equip, and work powerfully in people's lives. The Spirit's primary role is to glorify Christ, and these emphases and disciplines magnify His ministry by focusing on the person of Jesus Christ. As we notice, name, and nurture the presence of God, we walk hand in hand with the Spirit of God, trusting Him to give light to see, wisdom to apply, and courage to act as we honor the Savior He glorifies in us.

One of the dangers in the Millennial Generation is that these young people are used to virtual reality. Technology has advanced so much that computer games seem very much like real events. Their games make players feel as if they are flying a spacecraft, fighting aliens, making millions of dollars, and participating in almost any other excitement they want to have. When these games are finished, the kids turn off the computer and walk away. I'm concerned that some kids play so many of these virtual games that when they encounter Christ, they think they can have a "virtual spirituality." They can have all of Christ they want, but when they're through (for example, when He asks for obedience), they turn off and walk away without a pang of conscience or a drop of remorse.

I'm convinced that young men and women desperately want a genuine spiritual experience. Their culture tells them it isn't so important what that experience is as long as they experience something. We know where that comes from: the pit of hell! Satan is the deceiver. He wants to tickle our desires and promise us the moon. His counterfeits look attractive to those with untrained eyes, but they are the path of destruction. Just as the Holy Spirit's ministry is powerful in encouraging young people to experience Christ, so Satan is subtle and cunning in promising that other roads will take them where they want to go. Read the titles of New Age books. Look at the ads for New Age seminars. They tell people their lives will be changed, they will have new, deep meaning in their lives, and they will have experiences that will revolutionize their lives. The books and seminars promise what only Christ can deliver, but the hook is experience. That's the door to this generation. Let's enter it boldly with the experience of holding the hand of Christ with one hand and the unwavering truth of the Word of God with the other. These kids need both.

10

Hold Fast
to the
Truth

I walked into a meeting of leadership students of a church youth group. I wanted to talk to them about the authority of Scripture to bolster their already strong faith. I wanted to dive right in, so I asked them, "How do we know the Bible is true?"

Several students instantly responded, "We don't!" A few others looked confused. They were wrestling with the question, trying to come up with a positive answer. They just couldn't think of anything. Finally a sweet girl said, "Because it's God's Word."

I would have expected those responses if I'd been speaking in a biology class at the local high school, but these were the cream of the crop, the kids other Christian kids looked to for guidance. For several of them at least, the issue of the authority of the Bible is a foregone conclusion—in the negative!

PAUL VISITS ATHENS

I believe the youth culture today is approaching the scene Paul encountered when he visited Athens. Acts 17 recounts that part of his ministry. Paul "reasoned in the synagogue with the Jews and with the Gentile worshipers, and in the marketplace daily with those who happened to be there" (v. 17). A group of philosophers

began to debate him. The group was made up of people from dia-
metrically opposite points of view. The Epicureans were characterized by the statement "Eat, drink, and be merry, for tomorrow we
die!" They wanted all they could get as soon as they could get it,
and they reveled in drinking, having sex, and carousing. This
group also contained the Epicureans' mirror image, the Stoics, who
believed that natural laws governed all things, and wise men lived
virtuous lives based on reason. Today, *stoic* means "unemotional,
indifferent to sadness, fear, and joy."

Neither the Stoics nor the Epicureans understood what Paul
was trying to say, so they called him a "babbler." They took Paul to
a meeting of the Areopagus so that distinguished group of philosophers could hear Paul's strange message. They told Paul, "May we
know what this new doctrine is of which you speak? For you are
bringing some strange things to our ears. Therefore we want to
know what these things mean." Luke added this editorial comment: "All the Athenians and the foreigners who were there spent
their time in nothing else but either to tell or to hear some new
thing" (vv. 19–21). And they didn't even have afternoon or late
night talk shows! For those men, truth wasn't the object. They were
after entertainment, and listening to different ideas—the stranger,
the better—was their delight.

I walk into the bookstore and read the titles on spirituality,
which look like a reading list from first-century Athens. A zillion
different philosophies and gods vie for attention, and obviously
they sell pretty well! To the untrained or unwary eye, all of them
promise to make life better. They all seem to have merit. For too
many Christians, young and old, the relative merits of these false
religions seem just about as good as the faith of their fathers.

I have the sneaking suspicion that Paul felt in the meeting of
the Areopagus the same things I feel in a Barnes & Noble: profound disgust. But Paul was an ambassador, not an executioner. He
stood up and said, "Men of Athens, I perceive that in all things you
are very religious; for as I was passing through and considering the

objects of your worship, I even found an altar with this inscription: TO THE UNKNOWN GOD. Therefore, the One whom you worship without knowing, Him I proclaim to you" (vv. 22–23).

Three Greek historians, Diogenes Laertius, Philostratus, and Pausanias, described a plague that struck Athens around 600 B.C. The people of Athens offered sacrifices to their 30,000 gods, but the plague continued to take lives. The gods obviously were unappeased. The city elders grew desperate. They sent for a philosopher named Epimenides and explained all that they had done, and that the gods weren't listening. Epimenides concluded there must be some other god who wasn't represented by the 30,000 idols in the city. Certainly the god could do something to lift the plague, but they had to find a way to contact him. Others protested, "But we don't know his name!"

Epimenides reasoned that any god who was good enough to lift their plague would be willing to overlook the fact that the elders didn't know his name. He called for a flock of sheep to be let go on Mars Hill. If any sheep lay down instead of grazing, they would assume that's where they should be sacrificed. And they were. Immediately the plague was over. On those sites, the elders erected statues "To the unknown God." By the time Paul arrived in Athens six hundred years later, at least one of those statues was still standing.

Paul didn't tell the men of Athens they were stupid for being so open that they had lost any sense of objectivity. And it doesn't do any good for me to condemn kids who have bought the "tolerance" line and lost their sense of objectivity. Paul complimented them on being religious, and he found common ground in an obscure statue to an unknown God. He used the reference point to proclaim the gospel of Christ to the people, even quoting their own philosophers to make one of his points, starting from creation and continuing to explain God's grace, ultimately by raising Christ from the dead.

How did they respond? "When they heard of the resurrection

of the dead, some mocked, while others said, 'We will hear you again on this matter.' So Paul departed from among them. However, some men joined him and believed" (vv. 32–34). Up until Paul talked about Christ, Paul's philosophy wasn't so different from others they'd heard: a supreme God who intervenes in the lives of men. The Greeks had hundreds of gods like that. But sin, judgment, grace, and resurrection? Those were different matters. The Resurrection took the Christian message out of the realm of philosophy into history. Most of the council couldn't handle that. If it were true, they couldn't sit around all day being tolerant of every view in the world. They'd have to trust in one way, one God, and one message, and they'd have to obey.

THE WATERSHED ISSUE

The Christian message rises or falls on that one point in time-space history: the resurrection of Jesus Christ. The moral laws of the Old Testament are lofty and difficult, but they can be understood and debated. Other religions have similar tenets of ethics and morality. But the Resurrection makes our faith categorically different from all others. Paul wrote to the believers in Corinth, "If there is no resurrection of the dead, then Christ is not risen. And if Christ is not risen, then our preaching is empty and your faith is also empty" (1 Cor. 15:13–14). A sad fact is that our culture's view of the Scriptures has eroded and clouded Paul's clear, objective assertion.

UNDER SIEGE

"The battle for the Bible" was actually begun in the 1880s in Germany when scholars scrutinized the text with higher criticism and held that the Scriptures had errors; therefore, we can obtain moral truth from its pages, but we can't be certain of much (if anything) in it. In the early part of this century, men of faith confronted this challenge. They defended the authority of Scripture, but their label, fundamentalists, gradually connoted a narrow-minded, defensive reaction instead of a valiant stand for truth. Our challenge today is to stand strong, but **to** communicate in a winsome way, just as Paul did to the Areopagus. To the Millennials, we also have to validate the truth with experience—not because the truth requires validation, but because this generation requires it.

Unfortunately discerning who believes the Bible and who doesn't is often difficult. A movement formed in response to the school of higher criticism was called neoorthodoxy. Francis Schaeffer observed, "The heart of neo-orthodox existential theology is that the Bible gives us a quarry out of which to have religious experience, but that the Bible contains mistakes where it touches that which is verifiable—namely history and science. But unhappily . . . the neo-orthodox existential theology is being taught under the name of evangelicalism."[1] So to neoorthodox theologians, the Bible *contains* the word of God, but it is not the Word of God. Noble-sounding adherents tell followers that the Bible is a beautiful guide for their lives "in spite of all the mistakes in it." Of course, some of the Bible's stories are beautiful, but it contains many hard lessons of forsaking all, repenting, and obeying. When a person who believes the Bible is erroneous encounters these passages, it is all too easy for him to surmise, "Well, these are probably errors too."

Schaeffer rightly understood that the Bible must be our anchor that cannot be moved as we face the changing tides of culture, or else we will be storm-driven and our faith shipwrecked. He wrote,

> Does inerrancy make a difference? Overwhelmingly; the difference is that the Bible being what it is, God's Word and so absolute, God's objective truth, we do not need to be, and we should not be, caught in the ever-changing fallen cultures which surround us. Those who do not hold the inerrancy of Scripture do not have this high privilege. To some extent, they

are at the mercy of the fallen, changing culture. And Scripture
is thus bent to conform to the changing world spirit of the day,
and they therefore have no solid authority upon which to judge
and to resist the views and values of that changing, shifting
world spirit.[2]

If held high, Scripture can "judge the thoughts and intentions of
men's hearts" and guide wayward individuals—and a lost culture—to repentance, forgiveness, and life.

OUR RESPONSE

How do we help the Millennial Generation perceive and value
the truth of Scripture? We need to clearly confront the mushy
thinking about the Bible and the soft spirituality around us. Just as
Paul was probably disgusted but communicated truth in love, so
should we speak the truth boldly but with the joy of our own experience of God's love, forgiveness, and power.

Perhaps we need to dust off some of the old books by scholars such as F. F. Bruce and John Warwick Montgomery about biblical history, archaeology, and the New Testament documents.
Maybe we should dig Josh McDowell's book *Evidence That
Demands a Verdict* out of the attic and teach kids about internal
and external evidence for the authority of Scripture. Apologetics
has not played a prominent role in teaching Millennials to value
Scripture. Does it seem too dry? Then maybe we should think
more about passages like Daniel's prophecy that a decree would
go forth from King Nebuchadnezzar to rebuild the walls of
Jerusalem, and 483 years (69 times 7) from that date, the Messiah
would appear. Scholars tell us that that exact date is Palm Sunday
when Jesus rode into Jerusalem on a donkey to the cries of the
crowds, "Hosanna to the King!"[3] If that doesn't get your apologetics
blood pumping, what will?

We have to be careful that we don't let the culture dictate what we teach. We listen to the culture and we make sure we are relevant to the times, but we speak with authority from the Scriptures. I tell students, "I am going to speak very clearly and directly because I truly believe this to be true. You will know it is true as well when you hear me because truth takes care of itself. I'm going to ask you to give me a chance, to listen to what I have to say. Then we can talk about it. But really listen because you will be able to know that it is true."

THE HOLY SPIRIT'S VITAL ROLE

At that point I have to count on the Holy Spirit to probe the hearts of those who are listening. He is the One who leads people to truth. As I teach the truth of the Bible, I'm convinced that the Holy Spirit is using my message to change lives. If we back off from that conviction, our message becomes mushy in our desire to accommodate the audience. Then they won't take us seriously, and no lives will be changed. If we are consumed with pleasing the audience, we won't be effective voices of God. My message is, "I love you. Let us hear from God, and God will work." In communicating the truth, we care about them and let them know it. We unapologetically communicate the truth of the Scripture, and we trust the Holy Spirit to make that illumined and real in their lives.

Unless the Holy Spirit works in kids' lives, my efforts are worthless. I used to try to be hip and wow them with my cool. Even if that ever worked, it doesn't work anymore. Today I offer my love, my respect for them and their decisions, and the truth of God's Word. The Holy Spirit takes all of that, and He has to effect change in students' hearts. The older I have gotten, the more powerful I have become in that I have had to trust more in the Holy Spirit instead of my own abilities. I have nothing to say apart from the Scriptures, and I have no impact apart from the loving power of the Holy Spirit to change lives.

SHOW 'EM THE CROSS

I was at a conference speaking on the suffering of Jesus Christ, and I made the comment that Jesus Christ was not very good-looking. I asked a student in the audience to come up on stage and read a verse from Isaiah 53 about the Messiah, Jesus: "He has no form or comeliness; . . . there is no beauty that we should desire Him" (v. 2). I explained that Jesus was just average-looking at best. I went on to make the comment that most of us are not good-looking. Jesus had to die for everyone, not just good-looking people, so He came without a beautiful appearance. After that session was over, many students told me that they had never thought of that before. It meant a lot to them because they, too, were just average in appearance.

Kids are moved by simple things like that. The most powerful story you could tell is the Cross. I have been known as the one who tells the story of the Cross. There is nothing like the story of the Cross to move teenagers in this generation because it is so full of Christ's love and His willingness to be trashed to show His love. It is also very, very graphic and bloody. That depicts the sufferings of Christ more powerfully than any movie, any video game, or anything they have ever seen or heard. And the Holy Spirit works powerfully when we talk about the Cross, so they will accept Christ when you talk about the Cross. But even this generation who has seen everything and experienced everything will be moved by it. Kids love to hear stories now more than ever, and I always hope to be one of the best storytellers of the cross of Jesus Christ that this generation has ever heard.

No matter how smooth this generation may become, no matter how much information they have heard, no matter how secular they are, they—like all other generations—need to be loved. The love of Christ still compels them. When we talk about the Cross, we can address the point where they are aching, and the love of Christ can meet them there.

An Opening

The culture's penchant for tolerance undermines our stand on objective truth. Anytime we say, "This is what the Bible says," they respond, "That's just your opinion," or worse, "You shouldn't judge other people's beliefs." Passionate tolerance subverts clear thinking about (and response to) the message of sin, judgment, the Cross, and forgiveness. If all philosophies and religions are valid, they believe, then don't get so worked up over one particular view.

We have an opening, I believe, in the Millennials' lack of purpose in their lives. Even if they can find no cause to live and die for in the culture, we have one for them. If God's Spirit will penetrate this demonically inspired tolerance (am I being too harsh?) and part the veil of truth, then young people today will be gripped by the lostness of man, the reality of eternal judgment. Their preoccupation with entertainment and ease will be transformed into cutting-edge discipleship and service for the Master who bought them with a price. Is this too much to hope for? I think not. For one thing, the True Love Waits campaign has proved that kids today will respond to a challenge. They will commit themselves if the truth is presented and the offer is clearly given.

Communicate with Tenacity and Compassion

A Gallup survey reported that only 35 percent of teenagers can name the four Gospels. A similar percentage can name at least four of the Ten Commandments, and 86 percent of the adolescents who go to church do not read the Bible on their own. They perceive the life-giving Word of God as irrelevant, stiff, and pushy. How can this perspective be changed? Here are my suggestions:

- Be fiercely relevant. Make sure what you talk about is important to the lives of the young people. We've often focused on the hot topics of sex, dating, and drugs, and these are, indeed, important, but students want to know how they can really relate to God, what kind of purpose they can have for their lives, and how they can have meaningful relationships that won't shatter in divorce and disillusionment. And forgiveness is always a relevant topic.

- Focus on application. Most of us do a pretty good job of telling a good story and attaching it to a passage of Scripture, but I think application is the most needed, and the most neglected, aspect of Bible study. It takes extra effort to help someone see how a truth or principle makes a concrete difference in actual life, and it takes even more effort to demonstrate how someone can make it real in experience. I'd like to think kids are smart enough to make the jump from principles to application on their own, but they're not. That isn't an indictment; I couldn't when I was their age either.

- Use experiential teaching methods. As much as possible, avoid talks that don't involve the listeners in the exercise. The method described in the last chapter to involve students in an event in Jesus' ministry can be adapted for many uses. Consider plays, walks, meditations, and praying through passages. Remember, kids today need to experience truth, not just hear truth. That means you and I have to take an extra step or two in preparation to provide an environment that facilitates their active involvement.

- Center on Jesus. No matter what topic you address, keep Jesus Himself as the focus of attention. He personally is the One who loves, understands, and is powerful to meet needs. Some of us love theology—and there is nothing wrong with good theology—but let theology be rich and real as it describes the person of God, not just principles and intricate controversies that may satisfy the mind but not the heart. To be honest, women do a lot better job of being intimate with God. Guys, let's learn from our sisters.

I believe the Gospels will be the place we camp out most often in our time of communicating the Word of God. The images are so strong, the relationships between Jesus and His friends and enemies are so challenging, we will do well to paint vivid pictures of these encounters and put our kids in these scenes.

- Obtain Bibles they can understand. I'm not trying to step on anybody's toes, but some translations are just too difficult for young people to understand. They are used to images being spoon-fed to them on movie, television, and computer screens. Reading is a chore. Don't put up a higher barrier by having them read a Bible written for people hundreds of years ago. Today, several versions are both accurate and easy to read. Invest in young people's futures by buying these for them.

- Hemorrhage. As Dallas Seminary professor Howard Hendricks has often said, "If you want people to bleed, you have to hemorrhage!" If we want students to have a rich, intimate relationship with Christ, we need to have one deeper still. If we want them to value the Scriptures, we need to value these truths so highly that we treasure them. Like it or not, you and I have been steeped in the culture of tolerance and mushy thinking. Where do you and I draw lines in our own lives about the kinds of television shows, movies, and books we consume? "It doesn't matter. I can handle it. No problem." I've heard that a thousand times, and maybe you can, but what kind of example do we set for those hungry young eyes that watch us like hawks? No, I'm not trying to be legalistic, but I don't want my freedom to be used as a covering for evil either.

We need a renewed emphasis on the beauty and complexity of Jesus. Philip Yancey has paved the way for us by writing *The Jesus I*

Never Knew. We would do well to get beyond the simple answers and drink deeply from the well of Jesus' love, strength, and ability to deal with each person He encountered.

In an age of relativism, values have been reversed. Standing for truth is considered immoral; sin is acceptable; and condemning sin is the worst sin of all. In an article in the *Wall Street Journal* titled "The Sin of Forgiveness," Dennis Prager noted that "none of [his] pre-1975 dictionaries contains the word 'judgmental.' Today, judging evil is widely considered worse than doing evil."[4]

How much have you and I been affected by this culture's values? Probably more than we'd like to think. Like Paul, we need to clearly see the contrast between biblical truth and a culture's values. Like Paul, we need to have the courage to confront those values in the marketplace, the schools, and the highest council of opinion in the land. And like Paul, we need to do it in such a way that we are not on the defensive, but gladly articulating the grace of God and our incredibly attractive Savior so that men and women will be drawn to Him.

11

The Challenges
of Discipling
the Millennial Generation

We are in a transition period. The entertainment/knowledge model in youth ministry of the past forty years still works to some degree, but as the audience continues to change, it will become less and less effective. Similarly our assumptions about what teenagers are like are in transition. Sure, the same developmental issues are at work, but the cultural environment is shifting, flowing, changing. We'd better be alert! I believe three words must characterize our discipleship of the Millennials: *experience, connections,* and *trust.* These have always been important, but they were more or less assumed in the past. Today, they must be the focus of our concerted efforts as we love these teenagers for Jesus' sake.

BEYOND ENTERTAINMENT

Teenagers are entertained to death. They love it, but the novelty is gone. They increasingly gravitate toward video games, movies, and roller coasters that make their experience a little more scary, more sensuous, or more something. They want to go beyond entertainment to genuine experience.

As the family erodes, relationships become both strained and complex with half siblings, stepparents, and a proliferation of cousins and other relatives. And more is not usually merrier. Every holiday contains inherent demands pulling teenagers in different directions. The tension is in stark contrast with the idyllic commercials on television implying that each holiday should be full of love, trust, and harmony. Teenagers are crying out—or wanting to cry out but are afraid no one is listening—as never before for meaningful relationships. They crave genuine connections based on real love. This craving drives them to substitute sexual encounters and the many forms of escape when the pain of isolation is too great. Youth ministry can step into the void and become a surrogate family for these young men and women longing for love.

Because of all the broken promises, Millennials don't trust adults under their own roofs, in their schools, in their government, and in their churches. Entertainment and the conveyance of knowledge don't build trust. Only real love, consistent and radical, can build bridges of trust to these young people.

The challenge is for us to put on new glasses so that we can see with more clarity. If we insist on using our old glasses, we will see enough kids who haven't changed to justify our position. They are still there. They still come to our youth groups. But our insistence on living in the past will forfeit the possibilities of reaching the kids whose assumptions have already changed. Believe me, I understand how difficult it is to move into this new way of thinking and seeing. I was slow to change from LPs to cassette tapes. I held on to my cassette player for a long, long time. I was one of the last to get a CD player. And computers? I feel as though I'm being dragged along into the information revolution kicking and screaming! I want to go back to manual typewriters. At least I knew how to use them without having to go back to college for specialized courses in technology. It's easy to stay where we feel comfortable. But when we consider that we may miss an entire generation, it's not worth the risk.

DRIFTING TOWARD SECULARISM

A *New York Times*–CBS News survey of thirteen- to seventeen-year-olds confirmed some things most of us have thought about Millennials, but it also had a surprise or two. The survey found that teenagers have been secularized to a great degree by the post-Christian, postmodern culture. They accept sexual activity as commonplace. One fifteen-year-old said flatly, "People are going to have sex, and they should have protected sex. They should have the chance to prevent herpes, AIDS and stuff." But the majority of teenagers held conservative views on a wide variety of topics from God to politics to parents. Ninety-four percent said they believe in God, and strong majorities stated they never drink alcohol or smoke cigarettes or marijuana. Fewer than one in four admitted to having had sex, but 71 percent said "a lot" or "some" of their friends are having sex. Here was an unexpected response: those who said violent crime is the biggest problem facing their generation dropped from 22 percent in 1994 to 7 percent in this survey. Drugs were identified as the biggest problem by 39 percent of the teenagers. Fifty-one percent said they get along "very well" with their parents, and 46 percent said "fairly well." Nearly two of three said their parents were in touch with what their lives are like. Almost half said they enjoy the same kind of music as their parents.[1]

This survey tells me that the entire culture, not just the Millennials, is drifting toward secularism. Values are changing at all levels, not just with the teenagers. If not, there would be more antagonism between the generations. We have to examine our own commitments and stop the subtle drift that we may not even see unless we look more closely.

We may be appalled by some of the harder music our teenagers listen to or the sex- and violence-saturated movies they watch, but we need to be careful not to react by condemning them. Instead, we need to look past these cultural trappings and look at their hearts. We certainly don't want to water down our message to become culturally relevant, but neither do we want to come across as harsh and condemning.

GRACE COMMUNICATES

I often think of Jesus and how He made friends with all kinds of people. The Pharisees and Sadducees condemned Him for going to Matthew's party because the "undesirables" drank and partied. Yet somehow, Jesus made those at the party feel comfortable without condoning their behavior. He was confident in Himself and His message, and His love for the people enabled Him to look past their behavior and into their hearts. Do you think He ever called them to obey God? Of course He did. They heard Him preach the good news, they heard Him respond confidently to the religious leaders (who hated the fact that Jesus so obviously loved the tax gatherers and prostitutes), and they saw Him relate to people in every walk of life with kindness and love. They also watched as He healed the sick, made the blind see, and raised the dead. That'll build some credibility!

In every culture and in every age, grace communicates. Loving the lovely is no big deal. Anybody can do that. But embracing people who are unlovely is the mark of Christ. One of my favorite passages in the Scriptures begins in Mark 1:40: "A leper came to Him [Jesus], imploring Him, kneeling down to Him and saying to Him, 'If You are willing, You can make me clean.'" People with leprosy were considered the untouchables of their day. They were required to yell, "Unclean! Unclean!" to warn others of their approach. Those poor people were shuffled off to colonies where their flesh rotted away with people of their own kind. The images of the leper colony in the movie *Ben-Hur* are some of the most poignant and compelling in any film I've ever seen. The noses, fingers, toes, and other parts of their bodies died. The flesh was rancid, incredibly horrible. No one dared get close, much less touch one of those people. The man with leprosy in Mark 1 was one of those desperate people. He didn't make a demand of Jesus. He begged. He got down on his knees and said simply, "If You want to, You can heal me."

Mark recorded the scene: "Jesus, moved with compassion, stretched out His hand and touched him, and said to him, 'I am willing; be cleansed.' . . . Immediately the leprosy left him, and he was cleansed" (Mark 1:41–42). I can almost see the smile on Jesus' face as He reached out and touched the shocked man. Probably the most he could hope for was that Jesus would speak a word and he would be healed. I don't think that man ever imagined in his wildest dreams that Jesus would actually *touch* him! Isn't that what attracted you and me to Jesus? Isn't that what still draws people to Him? He is still willing to look past our rancid exterior and reach out to touch us.

Be careful where you draw lines regarding the culture. If you are perceived as negative and condemning, you will attract fellow Pharisees. You might even get a large number of them. But if you and I model the love of God and let young men and women see our hearts and our values, we can focus far more on our purpose to love Christ and win people to Him and far less on the external trappings of the culture.

Two Examples to Follow

Both Jesus and Paul knew the importance of modeling with their disciples. On countless miles on the road, in conversation after conversation, and around hundreds of campfires, the Twelve (and others who followed Him) saw Jesus live out what He preached: absolute dependence on the Father, passion for the souls of people, genuine care for the hurting, clear challenges for those who burdened people with empty religion, and endless patience with those who were a bit slow to comprehend. Jesus built trust with the people by living honestly and lovingly among them. He didn't shame them for failing. He was loving and patient with people who followed Him. If there is any question about His grace to the wayward, just ask Peter. He could tell us how Jesus went out of His way to forgive, love, and affirm their relationship after Peter blew it big time.

Throughout Acts and in his letters to churches, Paul demonstrated his commitment to people as well as to truth. He made sure he wasn't a burden to anyone, so he worked a second job to provide for himself. He clearly and patiently taught the Scriptures day after day everywhere he went, and he endured the most severe punishments and privations for his efforts. Many of us think of Paul as a hard man who was driven to take the gospel to the world, but we see other images of him in his tenderness with Timothy and his loving remarks to the believers in Thessalonica. He wrote to them,

> But we were gentle among you, just as a nursing mother cherishes her own children . . . We were well pleased to impart to you not only the gospel of God, but also our own lives, because you had become dear to us. For you remember, brethren, our labor and toil; for laboring night and day, that we might not be a burden to any of you, we preached to you the gospel of God. (1 Thess. 2:7–9)

The word of the '90s is *mentoring,* and rightly so. Genuine "under the skin" relationships are what Millennials need, not more entertainment and dry knowledge. We have the responsibility and privilege as youth leaders to provide environments where we and our volunteers can spend prolonged times with these young people. We need to structure our youth group times to allow for this more intimate interaction as much as possible, and we need to have retreats. All of us know the power of getting teenagers away for a few days, but the need is greater today than ever before. We need to find places where we can get away from the constant noise and the constant pressures so that we can get below the surface. It takes more time to get there than it used to, and it requires more intentional effort, but it is even more critical if we want to build trust with these young people.

THE NEED FOR COMPETENT VOLUNTEERS

Volunteers are indispensable in youth ministry. A youth pastor simply can't relate to all the subgroups in his community. I recommend he find a volunteer to work with the athletes, one to work with the intellectuals, one to minister to the party animals, one for the skaters, and on and on. The skaters don't care about kids in the band. They begin to care about anybody outside their own group only when they grow in Christ and are changed by His love. They don't understand anybody outside their group, and in the initial stages of contact with the youth group, they don't care.

Some youth workers refuse to value volunteers. They see their youth group grow to thirty or so, but then it stops growing because it's a one-man show. I spoke with a youth leader about this, and he told me he didn't really care if his youth group got any bigger than thirty-five. He was happy where he was. Maybe this young man felt comfortable with the size of his youth group and was afraid he couldn't handle the pressure of a larger group. Or maybe he had seen other youth pastors burn out from trying to do too much. Maybe he even believed that pursuing larger numbers was prideful. However, from my interaction with him, I believe he was focused more on his needs than the needs of lost kids in his community, and he wasn't willing to pay the price to see more kids come. If we're not willing to do niche ministries in the twenty-first century, then we need to go into some other kind of ministry.

If I were a youth leader, I would know that there is a certain group of students who are into the Internet, of which I know nothing at all. I could try to learn, but in the end, I will never be up to their speed to relate intelligently on their level. I would need to find somebody who cares about the Lord, about teenagers, and about computers—and let him minister to these kids. They'll still come to the larger youth group for teaching and fellowship, but this group of students needs someone in tune with them and their interests to mentor them. I have to be mature to find someone who can relate to that group.

A chief priority in modern youth ministry is selecting, training, and shepherding volunteer mentors. None of that happens by accident. Pray that God will give you men and women of integrity and heart who care about young people and who will make the time to get deeply involved in the life of one or the lives of a few. Select carefully. Handling the problems created by a poor mentor takes far more time and trouble than taking the time and trouble to ask extra questions during the selection process. It is much better to have a few really good mentors than to have many who aren't capable or don't have the time to do what the young people need. If we make a commitment to a student to provide someone who cares, let's do all we can to make sure that commitment is fulfilled.

Selecting, training, and leading a group of volunteers are challenges that require additional training and expertise for many youth ministers. But if we want to reach every segment of our community, we have to pay the price. I talked with a youth leader a while ago who was very gifted. He breaks his ministry into thirds: one-third he studies, one-third he disciples or mentors a group of kids, and one-third he spends with the volunteer leaders helping them develop their mentoring skills.

BEING APPROPRIATELY VULNERABLE

Mentoring and modeling imply that we are honest about our own struggles, at least to a degree. If we communicate that we have all the answers and that we don't struggle, trust will be shattered before it is begun. But we shouldn't "tell it all at city hall" either. Here are my rules of thumb about how vulnerable to be with students:

- Be open about past struggles with God.

- Be open about present struggles with God, only after having them screened by a trusted friend or pastor.

- Be open about past painful relationships, without using names. If your struggle was (and is) with your parents, be sure to have someone give you feedback on it before you tell students. You may be wise to talk about it in the third person.

- Be open about past behaviors only after screening. Again, you may be wise to talk about it in the third person.

- Don't talk about other people's trash. If you want to use someone's sin or problem as an example, be sure it is adequately disguised.

If you speak it out loud in almost any context, you can be assured it will be broadcast widely. Reeling it back in is impossible, so be very careful to think about whatever you plan to share.

BE AN EXPERT IN AFFIRMATION

Sarcasm makes for cheap, easy laughs. Don't stoop to use it. For any reason. Ever. I have a friend who is a youth pastor, and he has never used anyone as the brunt of a joke. People around him feel safe. They know they can say or do anything and not be made fun of. Perhaps some of us use sarcasm because it was modeled to us in our families or by a youth pastor, or maybe we feel insecure and we try to be on top by putting others down with humor. Whatever the reason, sarcasm may get a quick laugh, but it causes a long-term erosion of trust. Genuine warmth is harder for some of us to communicate than sarcasm or even truth, but it is the stuff of ministry. Find someone who is good at affirming other people, and ask if you can hang out with him for a while. The time will be well worth it.

In the context of intimate, supportive relationships, sneak some good theology into conversations from time to time. Certainly you want to teach well from up front, but I'm convinced that young people listen much more intently one-on-one, especially in the unguarded moments. Steep yourself in the love of God, His goodness and sovereignty, so you see His hand at work in the mundane, everyday events of life. That's what Eugene Peterson talked about in his description of spiritual direction, and that's what Henry Blackaby and Claude King said is the first principle in *Experiencing God:* to believe God is always at work and to see His hand in every event and every relationship.

ACTIVE INVOLVEMENT IN MEETING NEEDS

Another important part of helping students experience the depth and breadth of discipleship is involving them in service. The heart of sacrifice is vital to the Christian message, but it cuts deeply across the grain of the Millennials' self-focused preoccupation. Don't just talk about sacrifice and service. Get them involved. Put faith in motion, and let them see how God can use them. You might organize a onetime or monthly project of feeding homeless people in your community. You might tell all the kids to grab shovels and rakes and paintbrushes and fix up the home of an elderly person in the church or community. (Be sure to ask first!) You might have some students volunteer at the local crisis pregnancy center to run errands.

As much as possible, get the students away from the church and out where they can touch the lives of hurting, needy people. Use these times to reflect on Jesus' ministry, His priorities to seek and save the lost and heal the wounded, and the ways that the experience has touched the lives of participants. I've seen these experiences open the hearts of young people who have sat passively for years listening to our talks and being in our games and skits.

These activities take some planning and, in some cases, some guts to step out of our comfort zones. How do you think Jesus' disciples were affected when they saw Him touch the flesh of the man with leprosy? And how were they affected when He sent them out two by two to tell others about the kingdom? Let your students watch you in cutting-edge ministry, and get them involved too.

Peer ministry is only a short step away from good mentoring. As these young people are involved in rich, real discipleship, they will be equipped to minister to others. Peer ministry gives them a sharper sense of purpose. They no longer come to the youth group just out of habit; instead, they come because they have the responsibility and privilege of seeing God work through them in the lives of their friends. They don't all have to become evangelists (though the ability and willingness to tell their own stories are parts of their growth). Visual images and music are inextricably woven into the fabric of their lives, so let them be a part of drama and music. Also, they may be much more proficient on the computer, so let them be in charge of networking information about youth group activities through E-mail.

As young men and women prove their commitment to Christ by their faithfulness and service, consider involving them in the decision-making process of the ministry. You are probably already listening to their wants and perspectives, but you can consider letting them be more deeply involved by coming to a meeting of the volunteers as you plan the next service project or retreat. If this is successful, you may then consider having a student leadership team with specific responsibilities. Be careful when and how you elevate students above their peers. Jealousy is destructive to everyone concerned.

SPIRITUAL KODAK MOMENTS

If you ask a student who has been involved in a youth group for a year or two to tell what has been most meaningful, he will almost always describe a particular event that stands out. Students may forget our pearls of wisdom, our insights, and the products of our hard study, but they don't forget those striking moments when God worked profoundly and obviously in their lives or the lives of others. I call these "spiritual Kodak moments." They are indelibly etched in our minds and hearts, and we remember them for years and years. These can happen at camp, in a service project, in a witnessing experience, in a crisis, on an overnighter, or in an exercise in a small group or youth group meeting. Keep your eyes open to see what God will do to make the ordinary extraordinary. I believe He will do that more than we can imagine. My encouragement to anyone who works with young people is to ask God to give you insight so that you can create these "spiritual Kodak moments" for those God has entrusted to you.

In an effort to be relevant, some youth ministries are adapting their style to be more accessible to Millennials. They are laid-back, with many quick changes in the content and format, and they include lots of student involvement. Others are using traditional rituals to provide stability through a historical context. For example, one youth minister sent students out on a wild and crazy scavenger hunt, and they ended up at the local cemetery at night under a cross. The helter-skelter scavenger hunt symbolized the chaos in people's lives, but all of us need to end up at the Cross for peace and meaning. The evening ended with a Communion service with the elements broken and poured by the volunteers for all the students. The entire experience allowed the teenagers to be actively involved, and it brought home a deep, meaningful lesson. They experienced what the youth pastor wanted to communicate in a rich, real way, and God met them at the foot of the cross.

I believe the power and integrity of relationships are—and will increasingly become—the most powerful vehicle to take the gospel to Millennials. The spoken word needs to be communicated boldly and clearly, but with their inherent lack of trust, relationships open doors and make people receptive to that message. We also need to get out of our comfort zones and move toward young people who not only *are* lost, but *look* lost. It's easy to enjoy the holy huddle week after week with comfortable people, but Jesus came to seek and to save the lost. He went to them. He didn't wait for them to come to Him.

Go to the outcast kids, the deeply wounded kids, the fiercely angry kids, and the painfully withdrawn kids to touch them as Jesus touched the man with leprosy. I know what you're thinking: *Yeah, but that man came to Jesus on his knees. I haven't seen many tattooed and studded kids coming to me on their knees!* You're right, but the man somehow had heard about Jesus, or maybe he had seen Jesus from a distance. Somehow, in some way, Jesus made Himself available to people so the man knew that Jesus had something he desperately wanted. You and I need to get out there and relate to the outcasts and furious kids as well as the athletes, cheerleaders, and scholars.

NEW HEROES

It has been said that Millennials are a generation without heroes. More accurately they are a generation without traditional heroes. They settle for sports stars and movie stars. Perhaps now is the time to resurrect some heroes of the faith. Read a biography of Hudson Taylor or David Brainerd. Thumb through the biographical history of Christian missions from Paul to today, *From Jerusalem to Irian Jaya.* Read about John Mott and the Student Volunteer Movement from 1889 to the 1920s when 30,000 of the finest young men and women went to the world to share Christ with those who had never heard. Listen to Elisabeth Elliot's account of her husband, Jim, as he was killed trying to make contact and share Christ with Indians in South America. There are true heroes of the faith. Now is the time to resurrect them and let them speak to the hearts of today's Millennials who so desperately need them.

REKINDLE THE FIRE!

Don't let the message or your zeal be watered down by cultural relativism. Ask God to rekindle in you a radical message, a radical commitment, and a radical love for Him and for people. Francis Schaeffer saw the need for a ministry today that powerfully blends experience of Christ in the context of trustworthy, strong relationships. He wrote,

> If we truly love our Lord and if we truly love our neighbor, we will ache with compassion for humanity today in our own country and across the world. We must do all we can to help people see the truth of Christianity and accept Christ as Savior. And we must not allow the Bible to be weakened by any compromise in its authority, no matter how subtle the means . . . It is God's life-changing power that is able to touch every individual, who then has the responsibility to touch the world around him with the absolutes found in the Bible. In the end we must realize that the spirit of the age—with all the loss of truth and beauty, and the loss of compassion and humanness that it has brought—is not merely a cultural ill. It is a spiritual ill that the truth given us in the Bible and Christ alone can cure.[2]

12

Making the
Church Work
for Millennials

George Barna has said that today's teenagers are "without a start-ing point to find God." This culture lacks the strong, intrinsic reminders about God, faith, and godly values that past generations enjoyed. We have to provide that starting point for them, and we also need to provide the other points of encouragement so that their faith will grow. As we look at our ministry to this generation of young people, we need to ask two questions: (1) Why do Millennials come to church? and (2) Why do they stay?

LIKE A MAGNET

Everywhere Jesus went, people responded to Him. Like objects responding to a magnet, some were drawn to Him and some were repulsed. He was different. He was a separate category from what they expected. John recorded, "For the law was given through Moses, but grace and truth came through Jesus Christ" (John 1:17). People were familiar with the law. It taught that people had to be perfect, or they would incur the wrath of God. Hundreds of specific commands added to the original ten. The list of rules was incredibly demanding. It demanded perfection in every action and, in fact, every motive. No one, no matter how devout, could attain its goal. All fell short. The laws gave the people of God an identity and showed them they desperately needed a Savior.

Jesus attracted people in many ways and for many reasons. They felt His love. They experienced His healing power. They were fed from His hand. They learned great truths from His lips. But in almost every case, someone was repulsed by His grace and truth. When the woman with the hemorrhage was healed, Peter was indignant that Jesus would stop for a lowly woman when He was on His way to a synagogue official's house. When Jesus stopped to talk to the woman at the well, the disciples were incensed that He would talk to a Samaritan woman. (There is a theme here about women!) Jesus healed several people on the Sabbath, and the religious leaders accused Him of being Satan's tool. I can almost see the upturned noses of those watching Jesus as He touched the man with leprosy. I'm sure they whispered to one another, "Did you see that?" Grace and truth were very attractive to some, but awful to others.

Another reason many were attracted to Jesus was that He stood up to the oppressive religious leaders. They were so pious. They put heavy burdens on others while they refused to lift even a finger. But Jesus didn't back down from their power at all. He told the story of the surly brother (otherwise known as the story of the prodigal son) to show how the Pharisees and Sadducees were missing out on the Father's rich blessings by being rigid and angry. When they continued in their defiance, He called them a "brood of vipers" and "whitewashed tombs . . . full of dead men's bones" (Matt. 23:33, 27). Can't you hear the graced people's cheers when He said those things?

WHAT ATTRACTS THEM TO CHRIST?

What attracts Millennials to Christ? The same things that attracted the people of Jesus' day. I did a survey of several groups of high school students, and I asked them that question: What attracts you to Christ? I left space for them to answer. I didn't give them multiple choices to pick from. Here's what they said:

- Because He loves me and cares for me: 55 percent.
- Because He gives me eternal life: 16 percent.
- Because He's always there for me; I can count on Him: 15 percent.
- Because he forgives me for my sins: 10 percent.
- A scattering of other responses.

Experience, relationship, trust. That's what the young people were saying attracts them to Jesus. I asked them to complete a statement: In my life, I wish God would____. Their responses here, too, reflected their culture. A very high percentage, almost 40 percent, said they wanted God to give them purpose and direction in their lives. Millennials are in touch with the lack of purpose in their generation, and they want God to fill that void. I've included some of their responses here. In my life, I wish God would

- give me clear guidance.
- tell me where to go to college.
- give me more wisdom.
- show me my purpose in life.
- show me what His will is for me.
- make Himself more clear about the part He plays in my life and make Himself more understandable.
- lead me in the way He has planned for me.
- give me wisdom in all my decisions.
- make me totally content.
- speak to me more often and tell me what He wants me to do.

- be more up front with what He is using me for and the direction He wants me to go in.
- lead me down the right path.

Many of the rest said they wanted God to be more real to them. In my life, I wish God would

- stay with me and watch over me.
- say "Hi!" once in a while.
- keep me close to Him.
- continue to be my Friend and Father.
- stay with me and watch over me.
- communicate with me more.
- help me be closer to Him.
- make Himself more evident to me.
- help me recognize Him more in my everyday life.
- talk with me directly—I wish!—or at least give me definite answers to my questions.
- speak to me in an audible voice so I wouldn't mistake His call on my life, and I could actually hear Him say out loud, "I love you, child."
- help me desire Him more.
- love me.
- help me and my friends and family know we are always loved by Him and let us know that He is always there for us and He is the number one thing that we will always be able to trust.
- bring me closer to Him.

Of course, there were a few answers like this: "I wish God would give me the girl of my dreams!" Overall, I was very encouraged by the responses of the young people. They live in a boring and fragmented world. They long for purpose and love. Christ, and Christ's people, can meet these longings of their hearts.

WHY DO THEY STAY?

Once they enter our doors, we need to ask the second question: Why do they stay? *Group* magazine conducted a survey of 30,000 teenagers and 200 youth leaders to find the answer to that question. The youth leaders were asked to guess how the students responded to that question: 80 percent said friendships were the glue that kept young people coming back; 20 percent guessed that parental pressure was the main reason. These youth leaders were wrong—way wrong!

Fifty-seven percent of the students said they stayed committed to their church and youth group because it helped them grow in their faith. Friendships accounted for only about 10 percent. Parental pressure? A mere 4 percent. Here are all their responses:[1]

1.	It's helped me to grow as a Christian	57.1 percent
2.	It's the right thing to do	10.4 percent
3.	The friendships I have there	9.6 percent
4.	Habit	4.0 percent
5.	Parental desires for them to stay involved	3.9 percent
6.	Fun	3.6 percent
7.	I'd feel guilty if I didn't	3.4 percent
8.	Adult volunteers	2.4 percent
9.	It's teenager-friendly	2.1 percent
10.	My youth leader	1.8 percent
11.	The senior pastor	1.4 percent

(Reprinted by permission from GROUP Magazine, copyright 1997,
Group Publishing, Box 481, Loveland, CO 80539.)

They really want to grow in their faith! They are highly motivated to learn about and experience the love and grace of God. Many of us think we have to be the Incredible Skit Man to keep these kids entertained, but they really want a rich relationship with God. This reality shapes our ministries. We can focus more wholeheartedly on spiritual formation. They won't think this emphasis is being forced on them. They want it. And we can be much more intent on noticing, naming, and nurturing the presence of God in our ministries—and in our own lives—as we shift our ministry forms from entertainment to spiritual experience.

Students' desire for purpose and love can be both met and fed as we involve them in service projects. Feeding homeless people, helping widows and sick people, painting the classrooms of a private inner-city school, and doing a hundred other activities will give them the opportunity to demonstrate the love of God, to "bear one another's burdens, and so fulfill the law of Christ" (Gal. 6:2). And watch their eyes as they see God use them!

IF LEADERS WOULD LISTEN

The *Group* survey addressed another very important question. Teenagers were asked: If we guaranteed you that your church leaders would listen to you, what would you want to tell them? Forty-six percent wanted to be more involved in the overall ministry of the church. (That figure reflects a combination of the first two responses, which are quite similar.) Here are all the answers:[2]

1.	Find ways to get teenagers more involved in the life of the church	32 percent
2.	Give teenagers more responsibility to help make decisions in the church	14 percent
3.	Make the church a friendlier, more comfortable place for teenagers to hang out	12 percent
4.	Make church more relevant to my life	11 percent

5. Replace lecture-style teaching with a learning-by-doing philosophy   10 percent

6. Stop criticizing young people and start encouraging them   8 percent

7. Offer more fun activities for teenagers   7 percent

8. Get back to teaching the basics of the faith   7 percent

So teenagers don't want to be involved, huh? Wrong! But we need to be careful. If we involve them on committees and in any other significant ways, we need to value their input. One church put together a music committee to reassess the style of music in worship. They offered to let anyone in the church join the committee, and the leader was shocked when three teenagers showed up at the first meeting. For month after month, the committee met. The most faithful in attendance were the teenagers. When assignments were handed out, they took their fair share. And they accomplished them on time.

But from the beginning, the three faithful teenagers were subject to snide remarks and condescending attitudes from the older people on the committee. "You don't know anything about *church* music," one choir member sneered. When one of the young people suggested they try some contemporary music, she was met with the stern rebuke: "Do you expect us to do *rap* in worship?" The kids were stereotyped from the beginning. To their credit, they hung in there and weathered the prejudice of older adults on the committee. In the end, they contributed greatly to the committee. Actually their attitudes and responses were much more mature than many others' on the committee. They wanted to be involved in the life of the church, but they had to pay a price for that involvement.

RADICAL COMMITMENT IN A MUSHY WORLD

Although the vast majority of students today are mesmerized and anesthetized by the combination of violence and sex in the media, the lack of absolutes, the proliferation of knowledge at their fingertips, and pseudospirituality, I find some students who are more serious about God today than ever in my memory. They seem to be tired of being entertained. They are disgusted or disillusioned by all the New Age, tolerance mush. They want truth and love. They want to experience God, to know God, to love God. They want much more than games at youth group functions. They are radically committed to prayer. It is a phenomenon similar to the days of the Jesus movement when kids spent so much time in prayer. I get calls from writers for national magazines wanting to talk about this great prayer movement on campuses. These students want to pray, and they also want to praise.

Years ago, we used to have to pull teeth to get kids to sing songs to God, but that has all changed now. The prayer songs that they want are songs of depth. We still do praise choruses in our conferences and our crusades to build a bridge, but they really want deeper, more meaningful songs to experience God. The popularity of "See You at the Pole" is an example of this prayer and praise movement among students today. In group prayer, students find a place to experience God and express their openness with God. In the group they find strength to stand strong for Christ in an often hostile environment. And today, many kids are coming to Christ as a direct result of other students praying them into the kingdom.

A few years ago a student from Germany attended a camp. One night, many of the eight hundred to one thousand kids responded to the altar call, but the boy from Germany just sat in his seat. One of his friends got up and came to me on the stage. He told me, "My friend Heinrich hasn't made a decision for Jesus yet, and he has many questions. Can you help him?" I stopped the altar call. I sat down in a chair and asked for another one for Heinrich. I called for him to come up on stage, and I told the crowd, "Heinrich still has a lot of questions about Christ. Let's see if we can help him." I asked the other kids to pray for him. And they did.

We started all over again talking about who God is, how we

know there is a God, and how we can relate to Him. After about twenty-five minutes, this German boy bowed his head and received Jesus into his heart. The turning point in the conversation was the understanding that he had nothing to lose by asking Jesus into his heart, and he had everything to gain. With all of his questions, what would it really hurt for him to call out to Christ to save him? I said to him, "If it's not real, you will know it. But if it is real, you will also know it."

After all the questions and discussions back and forth, he was finally willing to give Christ a chance. He met Christ on Christ's terms. He admitted he was a sinner, he needed help, and he could not face God apart from being forgiven by Christ. The power of so many kids praying in the audience was electric for him and for them. All of us were moved by the experience of seeing somebody turn to Christ in front of our very eyes. They also were part of that experience because they were praying as the German boy was truly transformed. Even today, I hear from students who attended that camp. They don't remember what I said, but they sure remember that "spiritual Kodak moment."

I have been touched by the response of young people to the Paducah, Kentucky, killings in which a young man walked in the door before school began and shot several students who were praying together. Many students have called our radio program or spoken out at our events to say they, too, are willing to lay down their lives for Christ and live for Him. This kind of dedication is refreshing and powerful. I'm also moved by the great mission movement that has taken place in the last three to five years of students going on summer missions. The popularity of summer missions is just about to catch up with—if not take over—summer camps. It is increasingly difficult to fill camps, not because they're dull and boring, but because this generation wants to do more than simply hear about God. They want to hear about God while they do something positive and active. They want to be involved in something that will change the world.

Sometimes older churchgoers talk about "those kids" in a tone of disgust: "They use our building. They use our air-conditioning and heating. They spill things on our carpet every week, and they don't even tithe!" In many cases, the problem with getting teenagers more involved in the life of the church is not that the kids don't want to do it. It's a segment of the adults that won't let them, either by exerting direct influence or by building a brick wall of disdain to keep them out. Youth ministry is often segmented away from other aspects of the church. In some ways, this is inevitable. Kids are loud, and they need space to do activities.

BUILD BRIDGES

I want to encourage you to build bridges between the adults in your church and the teenagers. Get some of the leadership kids to participate in a committee or two, even if it is only on a short-term basis. Ask the teenagers regularly for their input on all aspects of church life. Don't let it turn into a gripe session. Keep it constructive, and do your best to make sure their concerns and suggestions are heard by those who can do something about them. If these young people see results from their input, they will be much more supportive of every aspect of church life, and they may even have a vision for being involved in a life-changing ministry when they graduate. The process of getting them involved can be a bit messy (especially if you don't think it through from the beginning), but the benefits are well worth the effort.

So how do you make the church work for Millennials? Here are my suggestions:

1. Realize why they are attracted to Christ. Tailor your content and forms to meet those needs.

2. Realize they are there because they want to grow in their faith, not just because they want to be with their friends or because their parents make them show up.

3. Shift your ministry style from entertainment to spiritual experience. Focus on spiritual formation. Select volunteers, and equip them with the skills to notice, name, and nurture the presence of God in their own lives and the lives of the students.

4. Use service projects on a regular basis (monthly, bimonthly) to put feet to their faith so they will see God use them.

5. Selectively involve young people in the life of the church. On a regular basis, get their input and report to church leaders. Also, do your homework to find out how to get particular young people to serve (even on a short-term basis) on leadership teams and committees in the church.

13

4-N Missions

Postmodern. Post-Christian. We are in the middle of a historic transition from a conservative Christian foundation to a culture with Christian tradition but little actual faith. Some friends of mine are missionaries in Europe. The transition in that continent is farther along than it is in the United States and Canada, probably fifty to seventy-five years farther toward secularization. In most, if not all, of those countries, especially in Western Europe, people still have some concept of their rich traditions of Martin Luther, John Hus, John Knox, and the Wesleys. The people there are not antifaith. They just see faith in Jesus Christ as irrelevant. It is my great fear that our culture is slipping into this spiritual emptiness. We have already pointed out that Xers are the first postmodern generation, and Millennials are a step or two farther into that cultural morass. To Boomers, the Millennial Generation is a foreign culture. To reach these young people for Jesus Christ, we need to employ the principles of foreign missions.

EYE-OPENERS

In the intriguing article "Finding the Eye Opener," Don Richardson, author of *Peace Child*, says that God provides every culture with an "eye-opener" to the gospel, a hook so that the people can understand the redemptive work of Christ. Richardson cites the different ways Paul communicated the gospel message to Jews, to God-fearing Gentiles, and to pagans. In each case, Paul used something in their culture to relate the message. In Acts 26, Paul was speaking to King Agrippa to defend himself against unjust charges. Paul told the king about his own conversion experience on the Damascus Road. Paul recounted Jesus' telling him, "I will deliver you from the Jewish people, as well as from the Gentiles, to whom I now send you, to open their eyes, in order to turn them from darkness to light, and from the power of Satan to God, that they may receive forgiveness of sins and an inheritance among those who are sanctified by faith in Me" (Acts 26:17–18).

The first step of an evangelist is to find the right hook, the piercing metaphor, the "aha!" concept "to open their eyes." Richardson notes Jesus' example of the encounter with the woman at the well in John 4. The woman was proud of her heritage of living so near Jacob's well, so Jesus used the analogy of "living water" to tap into her interest. In Athens, Paul used the statue to the unknown god as the eye-opening beginning point to communicate the message of the gospel to that culture.

And what is the eye-opener for Millennials? What do they value? What do they need? We need to be sensitive to the Spirit as we talk to each individual, and we can also tap into gripping current events, such as an accidental death or suicide or award, to relate the gospel. There are, however, some wider eye-openers for Millennials:

- They long for intimacy and connections because of the breakdown in the family, so we can talk about God as a loving Father or Jesus as the faithful Friend who never betrays or leaves.

- They long for something to live for, so we can offer them the greatest challenge in the world: to represent the King of kings.

- They are bored from being entertained to death, so we can offer them an experience with the living God.

- They respond incredibly well to the powerful truth of God's love found in the message of the Cross.

- Their consciences and the conviction of the Holy Spirit awaken guilt in their hearts, so we can offer not only judicial forgiveness through the Cross, but also the wild, radical love of an adoring Father welcoming His prodigal home.

- They want someone who cares to gently probe their pain and minister the compassion and healing of Christ to them.

In his conversation with King Agrippa, Paul drove home the reality of the battle for people's hearts. He recalled Jesus' words that Paul's task (and ours) was "to turn them from darkness to light, and from the power of Satan to God." Ours is a spiritual battle. The tolerance-laden mind-set of our culture downplays the stark reality of this warfare, but Richardson reminds us, "There is real evil out there, and it lies within human nature. And you have to be against it, and if you are not against it, the Spirit of God will not be for you. You will lose his blessing. The Son of Man has come to destroy the works of the devil and to deliver people from sin in whatever form it occurs."[1] Peter, the church's first evangelist at Pentecost, tied his message of forgiveness for the Jewish pilgrims in Jerusalem to the Old Testament prophecies. When he was older and writing to a much broader audience, he focused on the love of God shown at the cross. He made sure he was clearly understood by those who heard him or read his letters.

THE TRUTH, THE WHOLE TRUTH, AND NOTHING BUT THE TRUTH

A good missionary or cross-cultural evangelist understands the gospel in its original context and avoids complicating the message by putting his own culture's spin on it. Boomers need to take a good, hard look at what Jesus' message was and keep it pure in our communication. The stark beauty and the power of the gospel are founded on blood sacrifice. For generations, Jewish prophets and teachers heard God speak and tell them to set up specific rituals for cleansing. The most holy day was Yom Kippur, the Day of Atonement, in which the high priest went into the Holy of Holies to sprinkle blood from an unblemished lamb on the mercy seat. The sacrificial death of animals was a symbol of One who would come to pay for sins once for all. God would someday come in the flesh to pay the perfect price for sin.

Jesus came, preaching a different message from the judgment the people had heard for so long. Instead of demanding "an eye for an eye," He told His followers to forgive. Instead of enforcing empty ritual, He encouraged a genuine relationship with God, and He shocked the Jewish people by calling God, "Abba. Daddy." Jesus put the new wine of grace into the new wineskins of loving relationships. His life, His message, and His movement were absolutely revolutionary—so revolutionary that the religious leaders of His day plotted to kill Him.

The freshness and radical nature of Jesus' message and ministry can be the same today if we are brave enough to strip away our cultural baggage and allow the unfettered grace of God to be exposed. Do we insist on certain hymns being sung? Do we have hissy fits if the order of service isn't what we are used to? Do we blanch when a studded or tattooed kid walks in the door? In our youth groups, do we youth pastors and volunteers hang around those we already know and feel comfortable around when a new kid arrives?

Or do we go back often to the richness of the original message and uncover the original meaning so that we can communicate to this new culture of Millennials with the same unencumbered love, grace, and power that Jesus had and Paul and Peter communicated in those early years of the faith?

To communicate adequately to Millennials (or any other foreign culture), we need to understand their worldview—not only to observe what they wear and what they do, but what they value, what they believe, and what they think is real. To learn these secrets, we need to immerse ourselves in their culture, be observant, and listen intently to what is said and what is not said.

I remember the story told by a missionary to Zaire. He said the people there were hesitant to enter relationships with him and other Westerners. The missionary began asking questions, and he learned the reason for the wall of misunderstanding. A Zairean told him, "When you came, you brought your strange ways. You brought tins of food. On the outside of one was a picture of corn. When you opened it, you found corn and you ate it. You brought tins of milk. When you opened it, you found milk and you drank it. You also brought tins with pictures of babies on them . . ."

THREE STAGES

Missionaries tell us that there are three stages in cross-cultural experience. When a missionary first encounters the culture, he is enthused! The challenges are fresh and exciting, and the adrenaline level is high. After a while, however, the honeymoon is over, and the missionary experiences the full weight of misunderstandings, privations, and loneliness. During this period, many missionaries realize they have to hang in there, or they have to leave the mission field. If they stay, most make the necessary adjustments to the new culture, and they feel comfortable relating to both the old and the new.

In the same way, relating to Millennials can be exciting at first. Their lack of trust is seen as a challenge, even refreshing at the beginning. A little later, however, their intransigence is frustrating. We wonder, "What's wrong with them? Why can't they see the truth and believe it?" At this critical moment (in more ways than one!), we have the choice to stay in relationships, endure the long, hard times of listening, often with little visible results, and trust God to work in His timing. If we can get beyond this time, we often will see genuine fruit because Millennials will feel comfortable with us, trust will be born, and lives will be changed. This analogy between us and missionaries seems a bit strained because we don't have to load a trunk on a ship or hop on a 747 to go halfway around the world to find our mission field. It's next door. It may even be under our own roofs!

The Message and the Messenger

Seminary courses in apologetics teach us to find common ground with people so that we can communicate the gospel to listening ears. As we have seen, Peter, Paul, and Jesus all tailored their message to fit the audience. They didn't change the essential elements, but they used the images and hooks of each person or group to win a hearing. Find common ground with Millennials too. Look for values communicated in their music, movies, and games. Use those as launching pads for discussion. Look for the sad events in the news to talk about purpose in life, hope, and eternity. But don't preach. Don't force your opinions. Win hearers by asking questions, affirming perceptions, and listening—always listening.

Remember that your integrity is a part of your message. Your warmth and honesty go far in creating an environment for young people to feel safe enough to share their hearts. I think of the woman at the well. How did her conversation get to the point of a discussion about her sex life? Only because Jesus loved her enough to open a conversation with an outcast Samaritan woman. You and I don't have to have all the answers. To a generation with incredible resources of knowledge, being a know-it-all can be terribly offensive. They are looking for love. Understand their culture. Be a student of their music and movies, their fads and the trends that shape their lives. Identify with them in their searching by explaining your own search for meaning and truth and by indicating that you are still on that pilgrimage. Share your frustrations as well as your triumphs, your heartaches as well as the gems of truth and wisdom you have uncovered.

And communicate love. Don't try to become like them. They can see through a phony in an instant. They hear enough garbage that erodes their trust. Don't contribute to the pile! Love, listen, affirm, and relax.

Don't expect or demand Millennials (or any other culture) to lay aside their habits and values to listen to you. A missionary—at least an effective one—doesn't have the unmitigated gall to presume others have to change just to listen to him. A far better approach is to try to lay aside your cultural idiosyncrasies and temporarily adopt the worldview of those you hope to win to Christ. When you immerse yourself in their thinking, their desires, and their values, you will better understand the eye-openers in that particular culture. If your goal is just to dispense the message to Millennials, you can avoid the hard work of understanding them. But if your goal is to truly communicate, you have to take the time and trouble to understand what makes them tick. Then you will be able to speak to their hearts. Their eyes will be open, and many will come to the Savior.

What do Millennials value? I believe they are disenchanted with the emptiness around them. No, they may not be able to communicate that, but many are tired of having nothing to live for and no one to share life with. Their frustration and boredom can be brick walls, or they can be open doors. The difference is our attitude.

14

The Challenge of Parenting the Millennial Generation

Parents of Millennials are confused. These moms and dads are giving their children more time and attention than their parents gave them, but these kids don't seem to appreciate any of their efforts. It is a truism to say every generation of parents is uncomfortable with teenage offspring. Today, however, that statement carries even more weight. On the wide cultural plain, the efforts of parents are being counterbalanced by the shift to post-Christian postmodernism. Our parents might have felt awkward about Elvis and the Beatles, or Debby Boone and Andy Gibb, but parents today don't understand how teenagers can be so entertained but so bored, so filled with information sources but so unwise, so pampered but so untrusting of authority.

BOOMER PARENTS, XER PARENTS

Actually there are two sets of parents of Millennials: younger Boomers and older Xers. They have somewhat differing styles of relating to their children. Xer parents are typically more conservative than Boomers because they are the lost generation, the latchkey children, and they don't want their own kids to experience the same pains they felt. Xer parents are reacting to being neglected by the older, permissive Boomer parents. These Xers compensate by being attentive and making changes in their schedules and budgets to provide for their Millennial children's needs and wants.

A recent study by the Partnership for a Drug-Free America shows that Boomer parents, famous for their own experimentation with drugs, are paradoxically unaware of their children's drug use. Only 21 percent of Boomer parents acknowledged the possibility that their teenagers had tried marijuana, but 44 percent of the teenagers said they had tried it. President of the Partnership, Richard D. Bonnette, stated that "few [parents] sincerely believe that their children are exposed to drugs, that drugs are widely available in schools their children attend. Boomers—many of whom have 'been there, done that'—are surprisingly and ironically out of step with the reality of drugs in their children's lives." Other findings include the following:

- Ninety-four percent of parents said they talked to their teenagers about drugs in the past year, but only 67 percent of teenagers recalled the conversations.

- Children's exposure to marijuana doubled from 1993 to 1997.

- Thirty-three percent of parents said their children believe marijuana is harmful, but only 18 percent of teenagers agreed.

- In 1997, children were less likely to tell their parents someone had offered them drugs than in previous years.[1]

This study shows that Boomer parents are significantly out of touch with teen culture and the ones who live under their roofs.

PARENTS MATTER MORE THAN YOU KNOW

We have analyzed the characteristics of the Millennials: they are plugged in and have incredible sources of knowledge, but they are bored, without purpose, fragmented into niche groups, and unwilling to trust adults. How does knowing that relate to parenting them? I believe parents need to be astute students of the culture as well as their own kids. Hillary Clinton's book *It Takes a Village* speaks of the importance of community involvement in raising healthy, well-adjusted children. Community involvement certainly can help, but parents must shoulder the responsibility of nurturing and equipping their children, no matter what help they receive or fail to receive from organizations and agencies.

Many of us may believe that the peer group has taken over the primary role of shaping teenagers' lives. After all, kids spend time with one another at school, at the movies, at youth group, at the mall, at the beach, and everywhere else imaginable. A recent survey, however, dispels this myth. By a wide margin, parents still rank highest on the list of influences in the lives of teenagers. They are watching you! What you do (or don't do) makes a tremendous difference in their lives. This is both good news and bad news. The good news is this: it's not too late to shape the values and behavior of those you love. The bad news is this: some of us have given up. When our children turned sixteen and got the keys to the car, we emotionally washed our hands and turned them over to their peers. If you've read this far in this book, you're one of the good news people! Your teenagers are looking to you for guidance and affirmation. No, they don't always look as though they want your input! But they want it. Actually they long for it!

AFFIRM, AFFIRM, AFFIRM

The Millennials' lack of trust makes communication with them difficult, but essential. Find things to affirm, to appreciate, to praise—no matter how hard you have to look. A pastor friend characterizes his ministry as "transformation through affirmation." I like that! People live for encouragement, and they die without it. Become a fountain of affirmation for the teenagers you love. Look past the messy room, the rushed schedule, the unintelligible music, and the preoccupation with style to see their hearts. One psychologist said that teenagers need at least seven hugs a day. If they aren't getting them from you . . . In his book *How to Really Love Your Teenager,* author Ross Campbell talks about "filling up a person's emotional tank" with hugs, love, kindness, and affirmation. Teenagers' emotional tanks are drained all day every day by the sarcasm, competition, and open ridicule of their "friends." They desperately need their parents to consistently express love and encouragement, especially when they don't deserve either one! That's what grace is all about.

Many of us aren't able to fill up others' tanks because ours are bone dry. If you seem to see only the negatives and are unable to uncover the good things in your teenager, you may need a twofold strategy. First, find a trusted friend, pastor, or Christian counselor to talk about your anger and frustrations. Past hurts may be blocking your ability to receive love. Second, determine to find the positive things to affirm in your child. You may have to fight against your anger and cynicism, but search until you find things to praise in your teenager. After a while, the combination of healing your past hurts and looking for the good in others may lead to a powerful habit of demonstrating love to them.

Some parents today are compensating for their own experience of being neglected by being permissive with their children. We need to blend affirmation with developing responsibility in these young people. It has been said that kids need roots and wings. They need the stability of knowing they are loved unconditionally by their families, and they also need the vision, freedom, and ability to try things on their own. In overprotective homes, parents hover over the children to protect them, but this overprotection robs young people of self-confidence. The children then feel incompetent, so they become more needy, requiring more protection by the parents. This cycle looks like love, but it is terribly destructive to the children and inhibits their maturing into confident, strong, secure, wise adults.

Increase the responsibility level a little at a time, so the fear of failure isn't too great. Encourage not only success, but even the attempt. Be your child's biggest cheerleader, even in failure. Your goal, remember, is for your teenager to grow into a responsible adult. That doesn't happen by magic when he walks out the door to go to college, to get married, or to enter the workforce. Many books are available that outline the stages of development and the appropriate responsibilities for growing young people to tackle. If you have been too protective, expect resistance. Your child will have to learn that you won't always bail him out. And you will have to learn to keep your mouth shut, not always give advice, and not jump in to fix any problem.

Permissive parents can expect resistance, too, as they communicate new expectations of their children. The fact is that in many families, one parent is overprotective and the other is permissive. Instead of balancing each other, they react to each other's extremes and become more extreme. Both lose, but the real loser is the child who witnesses the modeling of poor conflict resolution skills in addition to the problems of permissiveness and overprotection.

THE LONG-TERM PERSPECTIVE

In giving responsibility to a teenager, develop an overall plan to equip that child for life. Think about what he will need to become a good parent, a good employee, a good spouse, and a committed Christian. Don't just sit back and hope these things happen. Be intentional in giving direction and freedom, so the teenager gradually assumes more and more responsibility as his confidence and ability grow.

Try not to overreact to the Millennials' culture as your parents overreacted to yours! Take a hard look at what you are modeling in your home: your values, your behaviors, your commitment to truth, your emotional stability, your sense of purpose, and your calm wisdom. Young people desperately want to follow someone they trust. Some that I talk to tell me their parents are the very ones they trust most because these parents have integrity. They walk their talk and live out the things they say they value most. Look at your checkbook and schedule. These reflect what a person really values. If your money and time are spent on accumulating things and escaping pain, then that's what your children will pick up from you as the way to live. If they are spent on the family and advancing the kingdom of God, this powerful message will be observed—and assimilated—by your children.

EIGHT PRINCIPLES

Here are some specific principles about parenting Millennials:

1. *Understand yourself.* Get some feedback about your ability to affirm and love your children. Find out if you tend to be over-protective or permissive, and also determine your spouse's tendencies. Knowing yourself provides a benchmark for making changes in how you treat your kids. It's never too late to change.

2. *Engage them intentionally.* Learn all you can about their culture, and make time to talk. Great conversations sometimes can be planned, but often the unguarded moments yield the deepest level of heart-to-heart talks. Look for those moments. Pray that God will open your eyes to see them. I'm convinced they are there, but sometimes we miss the cues. On the way home from a ball game, on the way to pick up a movie, in the kitchen preparing dinner, and in the other mundane moments in life, God can give us windows to each other's soul if we look for them.

3. *Listen.* If you use those precious moments to huff and puff and blow down the teenager's house, the next moment may not come until the next millennium! Ask questions. Avoid condemning or correcting. And listen. Kids are looking at the expression in your eyes and listening to the tone of your voice to see if your

words and your heart match up. If you say you want to listen but your voice has the taint of condemnation, the door will be shut.

A friend of mine has a teenage daughter. They have a deal. When she picks up that her dad's voice or facial expression is not consistent with his words, she tells him. He told me, "I don't like it when she tells me, but if I say, 'I'm sorry. I'll try to do better. Let's try it again,' the conversation usually goes to a much deeper level. I think our agreement gives her a deeper sense of trust."

4. *Ask questions.* Don't jump in with your absolutely essential, incredibly wise advice—even if you're right! Bite your tongue and ask a few questions. Remember, having the relationship is more important than forcing your opinion on your teenager. Win trust by being patient and asking the second and third questions instead of looking like a know-it-all. Pursue your teenager gently.

5. *Clarify what has been said.* You may want to ask clarifying questions such as:

- "How did you feel when that happened?"

- "What happened next?"

- "What do you think her motives were when she did that?"

- "This is what I hear you saying. Is that right?"

6. *Impart tools of decision making.* Don't overwhelm your teenager with business management techniques, even if they have revolutionized your life. Use the back-door approach. Find unguarded moments, and ask a question or two to help your teenager plan a little better. When he sees success, you can then open Door #2 and say you've learned some techniques that help you be more effective. But don't push! Leave your teenager wanting more. Little by little, teach him to plan, prioritize, and schedule his time to accomplish his goals. Talk about consequences to encourage your teenager to internalize what he is learning. If he notices how good decision making makes him happier and more

effective, he will be motivated to keep going in that direction. Of course, these techniques are learned best in the context of growing responsibilities. When your teenager feels the pressure of increased responsibility, he may be more receptive to learn and grow. Every step of the way, affirm effort as well as progress.

7. *Practice spiritual formation at home.* Make it a part of your family's lifestyle to notice, name, and nurture the presence of God. You can do this as a regular part of dinner conversation or perhaps as a debriefing time on Sunday on the way to church. You can ask, "How have we seen God at work in our lives since last Sunday morning?" That will also prepare each of you to pay attention to God and His Word in the services that morning.

The offhanded times may be the best to impart spiritual formation. As you talk about the important and the not-so-important things of your lives, make it a habit to look for the Lord's hand in all you do. You probably will be surprised to see His sovereignty, His love, and His gracious provision as you never have before!

8. *Correct sparingly; affirm lavishly.* Okay, I've said this before, haven't I? I want to say it again. Our teenagers are no different from us. We all need large helpings of love all day every day. We live for it. We long for more. The only difference is that some teenagers are "going through that phase" of individuating, developing their own, separate identity apart from their parents. Some of them do this gracefully; most do it painfully. They are exasperating, but they need to be hugged. They are incredibly obstinate, but they need our kindness. They are out of control, but they need our steady, gentle care. Most kids I know are well aware when they mess up. They usually don't need us to point that out. A better approach is to put your arm around him and ask, "How can I help you? I really care about you." That will do wonders for your teenager and for your relationship.

Do you ever put your foot down? Do you ever say, "No!"? Do you ever practice tough love to change the direction of a teenager's life? Of course you do when it is needed. If we practice these other principles, we won't have to resort to confrontation too often. When it is needed, I encourage you to seek the help of a pastor or Christian counselor to enable you to communicate with clarity and with realistic expectations. Quite often, the counselor will observe that the problems with the child may be systemic, that is, they reflect difficulties in the entire family's network of relationships. This is an opportunity for all of you to learn and grow. It may be painful, but it can be one of the most positive and revolutionary experiences for a family.

BE A STUDENT OF THE CULTURE AND YOUR CHILD

Your particular teenager may be quite different from the typical Millennial. Every generation contains an enormous range of motives, lifestyles, hopes, and dreams. But the environment your teenager is experiencing in school and in our nation is decidedly different from the one you and I enjoyed or endured. You need to know that so you can be alert and aware of the dangers and the opportunities.

The Millennial Generation is not the most difficult bunch of young people to come along in years. In fact, as a group, they are more withdrawn than we've seen in many years. They need a sense of purpose; they need strong relationships; they need role models they can trust. If we understand them, we can more accurately shape the environment in our homes to meet their needs and point them toward lives of true meaning.

15

And Tomorrow . . .

In *The Fourth Turning*, William Strauss and Neil Howe describe predictable cycles in Western history. From the late medieval period of the early 1400s, these historians see four distinct periods, or turnings, repeated every eighty to one hundred years. They say we are in the third turning now, a time characterized by an "unraveling" of the fabric of society as government and other social organizations lose their effectiveness to help people. The fourth turning is a "crisis." Cataclysmic wars, severe depression, and social upheaval are the characteristics of this last part of the cycle, such as the American Revolution, the Civil War, and the Great Depression and World War II. In each of these, the entire order of society was turned upside down. People who were the teenagers of each of these third turnings became the heroes of these crises, the soldiers and visionaries who brought order from chaos, peace from conflict, and established a new beginning for an entire culture.

CATASTROPHE?

Some authorities believe the economy will collapse shortly after 2007. They point to that date because it is when the wave of Baby Boomers will begin to retire and draw Social Security. The billions of dollars that are being pumped into mutual funds today will dry up, and that will trigger a downturn, which may equal the Great Depression of the 1930s. Others see the proliferation of regional bullies around the globe. Some of these, they argue, already have weapons of mass destruction, if not nuclear arms. Biological warfare has put mobile and dangerous bacteria and toxins in the hands of those who are willing to use them to accomplish their purposes. A single belligerent, unstable dictator could wreak havoc on huge populations and throw the world into a prolonged crisis. Still others point to global warming, El Niño, and earthquakes as the sources of some kind of global ruin in the next generation. All of these—and a host of other calamities—are certainly possible. At this point in history, the tide of events seems to be barely under control. It wouldn't take much for the balance to tip and the potential for crisis to turn into reality.

Winston Churchill espoused a "great man" theory of history. He said there is no history, only biographies, which tell the stories of great men and women who determine the course of events, not the other way around. Strauss and Howe disagree with Churchill, but then, neither of them is considered "the greatest man of the twentieth century" as Churchill is widely known.

Adding to this crisis prediction is the proliferation of prophecies concerning the Rapture and the second coming of Christ. The turn of the millennium has produced a renewed commitment to reach every person in the world with the gospel by the year 2000 (or the end of that magic year), and inevitably this enthusiasm for evangelism is tied to the anticipation of Christ's return. If the premillennialists are right and the rapture of the church is followed by the horrific plagues and privations of the Tribulation, Strauss and Howe will see a crisis like none they have ever dreamed of!

The disaster model of the future notes the cycles of the past as a basis for predicting the future. The cycles, these historians conclude, are as regular as clockwork and as predictable as the sun rising in the morning. They don't know the exact dates or circumstances of the crisis, but Strauss and Howe predict the beginning of the days of doom will occur in the years between 2005 and 2015. The Millennial Generation, so bored and detached today, will be thrust into a pivotal role in the crisis, and they will rise to the occasion to provide manpower and zeal to meet the challenge and establish the new order in the coming first-turning "high."

A MILLENNIAL AWAKENING?

A more hopeful model of the future is that God will use the lethargy of the Millennials' entertainment culture to create in them a yearning for more. Out of their boredom, leaders will arise who will infuse that generation with purpose and passion. A movement of God will sweep that generation, and God will use them to lead their peers and their parents to the Savior. The modern network of instant communications will enable them to disciple converts on-line around the globe. The wealth of knowledge and resources available on the Web will be turned to this purpose, and the movement will be reinforced by tens of millions of E-mails daily.

CRISIS AND RECOVERY?

A third model of the future is a mixed model. It predicts that a disaster is coming in the form of an economic collapse, war, widespread terrorism, an ecological apocalypse, or a combination of these events. The Millennials will rise to the occasion, but they will combine their civic and military zeal with spiritual passion. The results will be a new order based not just on fresh democratic principles, but on a foundation of love for God and a desire to do His will.

Predicting the future is stimulating and intriguing. I enjoy looking at past trends and current events and trying to find patterns, but no one can see into a crystal ball and know what is going to happen in fifteen years, five years, or even tomorrow. You and I can't control the future, but we can have an impact on the lives of teenagers today. Matthew recorded Jesus' encouragement to focus on today: "But seek first the kingdom of God and His righteousness, and all these things shall be added to you. Therefore do not worry about tomorrow, for tomorrow will worry about its own things. Sufficient for the day is its own trouble" (Matt. 6:33–34). Be a youth minister or volunteer or parent with eyes open to see past the dross of the culture into the hearts of these precious young men and women. Notice their need and their often-hidden desire to love and be loved and to have a compelling sense of purpose in their lives. We may not be able to shape the direction of the entire culture, but perhaps God will use us to shape the future of a handful of teenagers or even one teen today.

Our Role

The same factors that have stolen the enthusiasm and trust from the Millennials have eroded the zeal of many of us. The media saturation makes us couch potatoes instead of active participants; the rapid pace of life leaves us tired and listless; we feel stressed because technology is always a step (or ten!) ahead of us; and family life suffers from the pressures. Perhaps the most significant thing we can do for the Millennial Generation is to renew our relationship with God. David was in the desert running from Saul, who was trying to kill him. David had killed Goliath—for Saul; he had won many battles—for Saul; he had played music to soothe the spirits—of Saul. But Saul was jealous and wanted to kill him. In David's emotional and spiritual pain, he expressed his heart's longing:

> *O God, You are my God;*
> *Early will I seek You;*

My soul thirsts for You;
My flesh longs for You
In a dry and thirsty land
Where there is no water.
So I have looked for You in the sanctuary,
To see Your power and Your glory.
Because your lovingkindness is better than life,
My lips shall praise You.
Thus I will bless You while I live;
I will lift up my hands in Your name.
My soul shall be satisfied as with marrow and fatness;
And my mouth shall praise You with joyful lips.

(Ps. 63:1–5)

God has made us so that our souls, like David's, thirst for God. We can numb that thirst by trying to satisfy it with material things, accomplishments, or people, but the thirst remains. When we are quiet, and when we are honest, we are more aware of this thirst for intimacy with the Father. The habits of seeking other sources of nourishment need to be replaced with new habits of pursuing God. The old habits don't fall away. They must be grabbed by the throat and slain! I believe that's what Jesus was talking about when He said to "die to self." He was referring to our self-centeredness, our penchant for trying to fill the hole in our hearts with anything but God.

I've heard it said that we won't trust God until we have to. Today, many people are more wealthy and comfortable than ever before. The affluence of our day doesn't force us to trust God. For some of us, the death of a loved one or the death of a dream drives us to God. Our thirst is awakened, and we have the choice to go to the fount of living waters. But I am afraid that many of us are too complacent to sense our need for God. Strauss and Howe's crisis may be necessary to thrust us out of our spiritual lethargy. I hope not.

EQUIPPING MILLENNIALS FOR THE FUTURE

What do the Millennials we love need from us to equip them for the future?

- They need our spiritual authenticity. They are watching us. If we are complacent, we will not win their trust. They will look elsewhere for direction and hope, and those other places may not be reservoirs of truth and grace.

- They need our love. As we look past their failures and successes and love them for who they are, they will be changed. Love does that. But love always carries a price tag. It cost Jesus Christ His life, and it will cost us our comfortable habits, our harbored anger, and our cherished possessions.

- They need intentional direction. As much as possible, we need to expose ourselves and our children to events and people who value Christ and His kingdom. Christian camps, concerts, speakers, retreats, and godly men and women can be used by God to shape the direction of individuals, families, and congregations. In this day, we need to think more deeply about application of God's Word. How does the truth matter in our most fundamental habits and passions?

- They need mentors. The church (as well as the business community) is recognizing again how important it is to have accountable relationships. The wave of popularity of mentoring is one of the healthiest trends in the faith today. Many youth ministries are selecting volunteers with the skills of imparting life, not just thinking up zany skits or being in charge of games on Sunday night. If your church doesn't have a mentoring program for adults and teenagers, begin talking about it, read books and articles about how to set it up, and select wisely.

- They need heroes. I hope God raises up a Paul in every community in our land—someone who combines intensity of commitment with genuine love for God and for people. Paul was willing to say the unpopular things, and he was willing to comfort the hurting. He was, after Jesus, the greatest hero in the history of the church because he never quit trusting God to use him. Today, we need young men and women who combine these traits in their zeal for Christ. Their stand for truth will be just as unpopular in the passionately tolerant culture as Paul's stand was unpopular to so many Jews and Gentiles. Paul was focused on Jesus Himself. Not theology, though Paul was the greatest theologian of church history. Not missions, though he was perhaps the greatest missionary in church history. Not denominational politics, though his words of wisdom resolved the biggest questions of his day. No, Paul was in love with Jesus Christ. We need men and women like him today who will use the gifts and skills God has given them for the glory of God.

The future may be glorious or traumatic for Western civilization, but it can be wonderful for Millennials who know they are loved and have a sense of purpose. A friend is a child psychologist who is an expert on this group of teenagers. He said, "Parents and youth leaders will have done their job if these young people can say when they leave home, 'I know I'm loved, and I know God has a purpose for my life.'" Millennials may be different in many ways, but they, like every other generation, need us to give them those two gifts: love and purpose.

A GENERATION WITH A MEMORY

Back in 1971, I had a kid in my youth group who was nothing but trouble. I knew he needed to experience something that would grab his heart. He had heard clear teaching of truth, but he needed a jolt to get his attention. One day I went to him and I said, "Listen, you want action? Let's have some action." I took him downtown to the winos and the slums on skid row in LA, and we sat on the street corner sharing Christ with heroin addicts and drunks. He listened to me talk about the life-changing power of Jesus' love, but this young man didn't seemed at all affected by the experience. After he graduated from high school, he moved away and we lost touch.

Twenty-five years later, I got a call from this guy. He said, "I want to tell you something. I've given my life to Christ. I've spent months tracking you down. When I left you, I drifted far from God. I got heavily into drugs. I had gotten to the place where I wanted to kill myself. I was shooting cocaine and heroin into my veins. At one point, I had a gun in my hand. I was ready to end it all. Then I remembered that day when you took me downtown, the things you said about Jesus. I put the gun down and rededicated my life to Christ. I'm calling to thank you."

And I thought that day on the streets in LA was a waste! After twenty-five years, he remembered the simple truth about Jesus, and he responded. Twenty-five years from today, the Millenials will be in their forties and fifties. They, too, will be a generation with a memory. The question is, Will they remember that we told them about Jesus and gave them "spiritual Kodak moments"? That's our task today. Let's do it well.

Appendix

SUNDAY SCHOOL CLASS OR GROUP LEADER'S GUIDE

Sunday school classes and small groups can use *Saving the Millennial Generation* as a curriculum to stimulate discussion and application. Your goals for using this book may be (1) to help people understand the uniquenesses and dynamics of this generation of teenagers, and (2) to help parents and other adults relate more effectively to this group of young people.

This material will stimulate, challenge and, at times, amuse you and your group or class. For some, a study of Millennials is an academic exercise. They will be stimulated to compare one generation with another and see the similarities and differences. Many others, however, are struggling as they try to parent their teenage children. This material can be an open door for them to share their hearts and receive the encouragement and guidance they need. Here are some things to remember as you prepare.

ASKING GOOD QUESTIONS

Discussions live or die because of the questions that are asked. Questions can be categorized as leading, limiting, or open. *Leading questions* demand the person to agree with the one asking, such as, "You agree that our generation is better than theirs, don't you?" Trial attorneys use this type of question when they want a specific answer, but it doesn't promote discussion. *Limiting questions* ask for a specific answer and dare the person to be wrong, such as, "What two things did Jesus say in that verse?"

These questions may gather information fairly quickly, so they can be useful in the context of good discussion. They cannot, however, take the place of good discussion. Used alone, they may (or may not) obtain accurate information, but they fail to promote a relaxed environment that fosters discussion. *Open questions* are not limited to one answer. They focus on two things: *why* and *how*. These questions frequently begin with phrases such as, "In what ways . . . ?" "Why do you think . . . ?" and "How can we apply . . . ?" Quite often, people will ping-pong off each other, and the discussion will take on a life of its own. This is terrific—as long as people stay on (or near) the topic. You may need to reel in the discussion from time to time to keep it focused. That's not a bad thing at all. It shows that the people feel comfortable talking and sharing.

Learn to use limiting questions to set up open questions so that your discussion will be rich and rewarding. You want to create healthy tension in the group to stimulate people to think deeply. You may even want to take an opposing view and play devil's advocate to create some tension. If you choose to do this, be sure to tell the group what you are doing, or you could seriously erode their trust.

DYNAMICS OF A GROUP

The topics covered in effective groups vary widely, but virtually all groups that make a difference in people's lives have several common denominators. These characteristics create a powerful, positive environment that is a hothouse for learning.

LOVE AND ACCEPTANCE

When we take time to listen, we communicate concern and love. When we hug someone who feels down, we let him know he is not alone. When we share our struggles, we make it safe for others to be honest about their hurts too. Don't feel that you have to be the answer man who solves every problem immediately with a word of wisdom.

Listen carefully to people as they talk. Look at them. Ask them second and third follow-up questions to continue to draw them out. Doing that will communicate that you really care about them. Also, use the ointment of thankfulness liberally. Say, "Thanks for telling us your perspective," or "That took courage for you to tell us. Can we pray for you right now?" Your kindness and attention give you the platform to speak the truth to receptive hearts.

TRUST

Appropriate self-disclosure is one of the best ways to build a trustworthy environment. When you tell stories about your failures, successes, hurts, fears, and hopes, others readily identify with you. Be careful, however, not to tell too much or tell it too graphically.

Encourage others to talk about their dreams and dreads too. As people feel safe, they will see how the truth you communicate applies to these areas of their lives. If someone shares about a particularly explosive family situation, it may be appropriate to gently interrupt and say, "Thank you so much for telling us about your hurts. I'm sure many people here can identify with you. I'd like to talk more with you after the meeting. Do you have a few minutes to talk to me then?"

INFORMATION

People are looking for handles on the truth so they can apply it to their relationships and experiences. As you teach, use quotes from books, the newspaper, and periodicals to add punch to your class or group meetings. Personal illustrations or stories of others' experiences paint word pictures for listeners.

The Bible can seem very dull and boring when it's compared to the excitement of today's videos and movies. And too often, we who teach the Bible contribute to this perception because we don't make these life-changing truths understandable or relevant to our listeners. Help people identify with the truth of the Scriptures by asking them open questions, such as, "How would you have felt in this situation? What would you have done?" or "What would Jesus do in this situation if He were here today?" Invite them to respond, but you don't need to comment on the validity of each response. Simply thank each person for his contribution and summarize at the end.

HOPE

Your class's or group's environment of love, trust, and truth provides hope and encouragement. Think of times when you felt confused and discouraged. When someone believed in you, you probably felt both surprised and strengthened! Struggling people need to be reminded that the Lord is strong and loving. He loves them deeply and desires their best. Though they may not understand their situations, He does.

Group leaders and teachers have the privilege of giving hope to these needy people:

- In the face of confusion, we can encourage them to make good decisions.

- In the face of weakness, we can help them to be strong.

- In the face of despair, we can tell them there is life on the other side of the present problem.

- In the face of guilt, we can share the forgiveness of Jesus Christ.

- In the face of bitterness, we can teach them to forgive others.

Be careful, however, not to overpromise. The Lord never promised to protect His children from all problems or bail us out. He promised to be with us in the middle of our struggles and to give us wisdom and strength to do His will.

LIMITATIONS

Though support groups encourage a deep level of openness and vulnerability, there are limits to a leader's training and time to deal effectively with the problems that surface. Some mistakenly think that they need to resolve every problem that comes up in the class or group, but this overwhelming sense of responsibility leads to burnout for the leader as he is driven to fix the problems in many people's lives, or, in contrast, it can lead to a denial that there are any significant problems at all. Neither is productive.

Before problems arise, be aware of the limits of your training, skills, and time to be able to deal with complex individual and family problems that people bring up in the group. Develop relationships with competent counselors and agencies in the community instead of playing a counselor's role. These professionals are trained to handle the complex and dynamic struggles in individuals and families. You can request to be informed of progress when a person is referred. Be sure, however, to do your homework so that you know the expertise and spiritual persuasion of the person to whom you refer someone.

Managing Difficulties

From time to time, even the best groups have difficulties. Learn to spot them early and head them off at the pass before they become big problems. Here are some common difficulties to watch for:

- Excessive talkers
- Silent, withdrawn people
- Conflicts between group members
- People taking the discussion on "rabbit trails"
- People jumping in to give advice when others voice a problem

Format

There are several ways you can use this book in your group or class:

1. Every person in the group can obtain a copy of the book and read along to be prepared for the next week's discussion. This method equips each person to participate fully in the conversations.

2. Someone can read the chapters that coincide with each week's content and give a brief overview before the discussion begins.

3. You can teach the material, then open it up to discussion after you have communicated the pertinent points. It is possible to teach one week, then discuss it the next.

Each format has pros and cons. Choose the one that's right for your class or group so that each person can get the most out of the content.

Six Sessions

Six weeks of content will allow you to focus on the major aspects of *Saving the Millennial Generation*. You may want to take longer if discussion is particularly rich and meaningful.

Each week will have an assignment. You will want to provide the books a week or two ahead of time and ask people to read Chapters 1 and 2 in preparation for the first week's discussion.

Week 1

Give a brief overview of the book, and tell why you have chosen it as a curriculum for the group or class.

PURPOSE:
- To understand the distinctive nature of each generation.

• To understand the major shift toward postmodernism and a post-Christian culture.

HOOK:

Ask the people to form groups of four or five. Then ask them to name five things that are the same today as when they were sixteen years old, and name five things that are different. Let someone from each group share their responses.

OVERVIEW:

1. Go over the characteristics of each of the generations from Boomers to Millennials.
2. Explain postmodernism.
3. Explain post-Christian.
   (Read any short quotes from the book that support your points.)

QUESTIONS:

1. Do you agree with the assessment that we are moving into a post-modern, post-Christian society? Why or why not?
2. How are Millennials different from your generation? How are they similar?
3. Do you agree with the author's characterization of Millennials? Why or why not?
4. What words would you use to characterize the Millennial Generation?
5. What are some examples of institutional weakness today?
6. What was going on in our culture when you were sixteen years old?

SO WHAT?

1. How does this analysis of Millennials affect how you look at them and the news reports about them?
2. How does this analysis help you understand the Millennials under your roof?

ASSIGNMENT:

Read Chapter 3 for next week.

WEEK 2

PURPOSE:

• To understand the changes in the culture over the last forty to fifty years.

- To recognize the strong currents going on in the Millennial Generation.

HOOK:

Divide the class or group into Boomers, Xers, and Millennials. Ask, Where were you when:

- John Kennedy was killed?
- John Lennon was killed?
- Princess Diana was killed?

Let them share with one another for a few minutes. ("I wasn't born yet" is a valid response that will help the group realize how different their experiences have been.)

Or ask, "Where were you when Elvis went into the army? What was your favorite Elvis song?"

OVERVIEW:

Explain that today's lesson is designed to help us understand the changes in popular culture over the past forty or fifty years. We'll reminisce, and we'll have a few laughs, but ultimately we want to see how different the youth culture is today from the Boomer and Xer teenage years.

QUESTIONS:

Ask each group (Boomers, Xers, and Millennials—if no Millennials are present, ask the entire group for their input to identify items for this age-group) to tell:

1. What songs, singers, and groups did you enjoy when you were sixteen?
2. What comedies did you watch on television?
3. What dramas did you watch?
4. What movies were your favorites when you were sixteen?
5. How prevalent and how open was sex?
6. What did drug use mean when you were sixteen?
7. What was advanced technology when you were sixteen?

SO WHAT?

1. List (on a chalkboard or overhead projector or piece of paper) ways the culture has changed from when you were sixteen until today.
2. Does understanding this give you more compassion for today's Millennials? Why or why not?

ASSIGNMENT:

Read Chapters 4 through 7 for next week.

WEEK 3

PURPOSE:

- To identify and describe the four main characteristics of the Millennial Generation: unwillingness to trust adults; information without wisdom; erosion of absolutes; and isolation, fragmentation, and drift.

HOOK:

Form groups of three. What words best characterize the Millennial Generation? Let each small group share answers with the whole group.

OVERVIEW:

This lesson explores the four main characteristics of the Millennial Generation. We want to examine what these are, how they came to be, and what they mean as we try to relate to today's young people.

QUESTIONS:

1. What are some reasons (legitimate reasons) today's young people are reluctant to trust adults?
2. How do the erosion of absolutes and the lack of a defining purpose affect Millennials' ability to trust?
3. Do today's teenagers know more than we did when we were their age? Explain your answer.
4. What are some examples of their "information without wisdom"?
5. How have you seen absolutes erode in the last twenty years or so?
6. How do movies such as *Contact* and/or education in public schools reflect and contribute to the erosion of absolutes?
7. What does fragmentation look like in the youth culture?
8. What are some causes of isolation, fragmentation, and drift?
9. Describe the interconnection of these four factors. How do they shape one another?

SO WHAT?

1. What is going on in your home on a daily or weekly basis that contributes to distrust, information without wisdom, the erosion of truth, and isolation?
2. What is going on in your church and your schools that contributes to these things?

ASSIGNMENT:

Read Chapters 8 through 10 for next week.

WEEK 4

PURPOSE:

> • To help the group or class understand how to communicate better with Millennials.

HOOK:

Form groups of three or four. Ask them to share their responses to these questions: "When was a time that you felt closest to God? What happened then?"

Ask several people to share with the whole group.

OVERVIEW:

The underlying cognitive and spiritual framework for Millennials is different from that of earlier generations. Their values are different, their spirituality is more intense but less focused, and they shy away from absolute truth.

QUESTIONS:

1. In what ways is communicating with Millennials like speaking a foreign language?

2. What difference does it make to you when someone condemns you? Accommodates you? Empathizes with you? Be specific.

3. What does it mean to Millennials to be "spiritual"?

4. Describe the differences between traditional youth ministry models and the spiritual formation model. Which are you more comfortable with? Why?

5. How have you seen the Lord at work in your life in the past week? (Notice, name, and nurture the presence of God.)

6. How can we help a relativistic youth culture value truth?

7. We have said that experience is vitally important to today's teenagers, even more than truth. How can experience be an open door to finding truth? How can it be a dead end? What factors might make the difference in these two opposite results?

SO WHAT?

Work it into your schedule this week for you and your family to notice, name, and nurture the presence of God. Plan a time to journal and to ask at mealtimes or in some other way, "How do I (or we) see God at work?"

ASSIGNMENT:

Read Chapters 11 through 13 for next week.

WEEK 5

PURPOSE:

> • To identify the church's role in reaching and discipling Millennials.

HOOK:

> Form groups of three or four. Ask, "Why do teenagers stay in church?" Let each group discuss this and then report to the whole group.

OVERVIEW:

> We need a clear understanding of how to reach and disciple Millennials so that our efforts can be most effective.

QUESTIONS:

1. Who are (or have been) the mentors in your spiritual journey? What difference have these people made in your life?

2. How can service play a key role in shaping teenagers' spiritual experience? What are some service projects available to your youth group?

3. Look at the survey results of why teenagers come to church and why they stay. Are any of them surprising to you? Why or why not?

4. What are some specific ways teenagers can get more involved in the life of your church?

5. Who will resist that involvement? (No names, please!) How will you overcome that resistance?

6. What are some possible eye-openers for sharing the gospel with Millennials?

7. Examine the principles of foreign missions. Do these apply to reaching today's teenagers? Why or why not?

SO WHAT?

> What are some specific things you can do to make the church experience a richer time for Millennials? Consider how to welcome them, provide genuine spiritual experiences, mentor them, provide service projects, and get them involved in planning and organizing and reaching others.

ASSIGNMENT:

> Read Chapters 14 and 15 for next week.

WEEK 6

PURPOSE:

> • To identify the role of parents in shaping the lives of Millennials.

- To examine the possibilities of the future.

HOOK:

Form groups of three or four. Ask, "What frustrates you most about today's teenagers? What thrills you most about them?" Let someone from each group share with the whole group.

OVERVIEW:

Parents have always played, and continue to play, the key role in shaping the lives of their children. The challenges of parenting Millennials are great. We need specific direction, courage, and the power of God to equip us to be effective.

QUESTIONS:

1. Describe the appropriate blend of affirmation and responsibility. How can you tell when each side is too much?

2. How does understanding yourself help you be a better parent?

3. Give specific suggestions for how each of us parents can
   - engage intentionally.
   - listen.
   - ask questions.
   - clarify responses.
   - impart tools for decision making.
   - encourage spiritual formation at home.

4. What impact would it make on the teenager in your life if you corrected sparingly and affirmed lavishly?

5. Which model of the future do you think is most plausible? Why?

6. How can you be prepared to be the best parent for your Millennial you can be?

SO WHAT?

1. What are three specific application points you will implement as a result of this study?

2. When will you do them? What is the process? What resources do you need? How will you know if they are successful?

ASSIGNMENT:

What is the next step for you? For this class? What books do you need to read? What resources do you need to help you accomplish your goal of ministering or parenting people in the Millennial Generation?

Notes

CHAPTER 1

1. William Strauss and Neil Howe, *The Fourth Turning* (New York: Broadway Books, 1997), 137.

2. Paul Rogat Loeb, *Generation at the Crossroads* (New Brunswick, N.J.: Rutgers University Press, 1994), 51.

3. Tim Celek and Dieter Zander, *Inside the Soul of a New Generation* (Grand Rapids: Zondervan, 1996), 31.

4. "Cultural Impact," *Group*, September-October 1994, 36–38.

CHAPTER 2

1. Jimmy Long, *Generating Hope* (Downers Grove, Ill.: InterVarsity Press, 1997), 62.

2. Vaclav Havel, "Adrift in a Post-Modern World," *Charlotte Observer*, 24 July 1994, quoted in Long, *Generating Hope*, 68.

3. Adapted from Long, *Generating Hope*, 69.

4. F. L. Cross, ed., *Oxford Dictionary of the Christian Church* (London: Oxford Press, 1958), 104–5.

5. Francis A. Schaeffer, *The Great Evangelical Disaster* (Westchester, Ill.: Crossway, 1984), 29.

6. Jim DeBrosse, "The Y's Have It," *Houston Chronicle*, 17 February 1998.

7. William Strauss and Neil Howe, *The Fourth Turning* (New York: Broadway Books, 1997), 247, emphasis in original.

8. Steven J. Novak, *The Rights of Youth: American Colleges and Student Revolt, 1798–1815* (Cambridge, Mass.: Harvard, 1997), 17–25.

CHAPTER 3

1. Study cited in *Houston Chronicle*, 17 April 1998.

2. "Protecting Adolescents from Harm," *Journal of the American Medical Association*, 10 September 1997, 830.

3. From "Facts," the Medical Institute for Sexual Health, Austin, Texas, October 1996.

4. Rebecca A. Maynard, ed., *Kids Having Kids,* A Robin Hood Foundation Special Report on the Costs of Adolescent Childbearing.

5. Thomas R. Eng and William T. Butler, eds., *The Hidden Epidemic* (Washington, D.C.: Institute of Medicine, National Academy Press, 1997), 36–37.

6. Quoted in Les Parrott III, *Helping the Struggling Adolescent* (Grand Rapids: Zondervan, 1993), 244.

7. "Protecting Adolescents from Harm," *Journal of the American Medical Association,* 830.

8. Reklis D. Fuchs V, "The Status of American Children," *Science,* 1992, 41–46.

9. Cited in *Houston Chronicle,* 3 April 1998.

10. "Protecting Adolescents from Harm," *Journal of the American Medical Association,* 829.

11. Cited in "Smoking Rates Up 'Dramatically' in Films," *Reuter News,* 3 March 1998.

12. Compiled from the Computer Museum of America, Coleman College, La Mesa, California; Robert X. Cringel, *Triumph of the Nerds: A History of the Computer;* Robert Hobbes Zakon, Hobbes's Internet Timeline v2.1, the MITRE Corporation.

13. Compiled from *The State of America's Children Yearbook 1997,* Children's Defense Fund.

CHAPTER 4

1. George Barna, *The Invisible Generation* (Glendale: Barna Research Group, 1992), 81.

2. Alec Gallup and Lydia Saad, Gallup Poll, "Public Concerned, Not Alarmed About Global Warming," 1997.

3. Paul Greenberg, "Clinton Relying on One Excuse After Another," *Houston Chronicle,* 11 March 1998.

4. Jonathan Yardley, "The Larger Significance of Michael Jordan: What Do Our Heroes Show Us About Ourselves?" *Sky,* February 1998, 46–50.

CHAPTER 5

1. Jeannie Kever, "Online, Out of Trouble," *Houston Chronicle,* 24 February 1998.

2. Ibid.

CHAPTER 6

1. Francis A. Schaeffer, *The Great Evangelical Disaster* (Westchester, Ill.: Crossway, 1984), 47.

2. Barna Research Group, 1994 survey of churched and unchurched youths, cited in Josh McDowell and Bob Hostetler, *Right from Wrong* (Dallas: Word, 1994), 18.

CHAPTER 7

1.   Netforum, "Private Optimism, Public Pessimism," 20 February 1998.
2.   Gallup Poll, "The State of Disunion," 1996 Survey of American Political Culture.
3.   William Strauss and Neil Howe, *The Fourth Turning* (New York: Broadway Books, 1997), 249.
4.   Joan Ryan, "A Painful Statement of Self-Identity," *San Francisco Chronicle,* 30 October 1997.
5.   From research by Teenage Research Unlimited, Northbrook, Illinois.
6.   "The Y's Have It," *Houston Chronicle,* 17 February 1998.

CHAPTER 8

1.   William Strauss and Neil Howe, *The Fourth Turning* (New York: Broadway Books, 1997), 134.

CHAPTER 9

1.   Cited in Wendy Murray Zoba, "The Class of '00," *Christianity Today,* 3 February 1997, 18f.
2.   Eugene Peterson, *Working the Angles: The Shape of Pastoral Integrity* (Grand Rapids: Eerdmans, 1987), 150.
3.   Henry Blackaby and Claude King, *Experiencing God* (Nashville, Tenn.: LifeWay Press, 1990).

CHAPTER 10

1.   Francis A. Schaeffer, *The Great Evangelical Disaster* (Westchester, Ill.: Crossway, 1984), 49–50.
2.   Ibid., 61.
3.   Josh McDowell, *Evidence That Demands a Verdict* (San Bernardino: Here's Life, 1986), 173.
4.   Dennis Prager, "The Sin of Forgiveness," *Wall Street Journal,* 15 December 1997.

CHAPTER 11

1.   *New York Times*–CBS News Survey, cited in *Houston Chronicle,* 28 April 1998.
2.   Francis A. Schaeffer, *The Great Evangelical Disaster* (Westchester, Ill.: Crossway, 1984), 39–40.

CHAPTER 12

1.   Rick Lawrence, "Why Kids Stay in Church," *Group,* September-October 1997, 23–26.
2.   Ibid., 25.

CHAPTER 13

1.   Don Richardson, "Finding the Eye Opener," in *Perspectives on the World Christian Movement* (Pasadena: William Carey Library, 1981), 421–27.

CHAPTER 14

1.   Cited in *Houston Chronicle,* 13 April 1998, 1.

About the Author

DAWSON MCALLISTER speaks to more than 100,000 young people each year. He offers a wide range of materials to young people, parents, and youth workers through his events and direct mailings. In addition, his weekly radio broadcast, *Dawson McAllister Live,* is heard on radio affiliates across the nation and is one of the fastest-growing radio programs in the country.

After studying at Bethel College and Talbot Seminary, McAllister started a coffeehouse ministry to thousands of runaways in southern California. Later he founded the Dawson McAllister Asociation, which he still leads.

McAllister is married with two sons and lives on a farm outside Nashville, Tennessee.